SERIES EDITOR: TONY HOL

OSPREY AIRCRAFT OF THE

'Down to Ea. ...
Strafing Aces of the
Eighth Air Force

by William N Hess

OSPREY
PUBLISHING

Front cover
'See you in a few days', were the last known words of one of the Eighth Air Force's most respected fighter leaders, and its leading strafing ace. But Lt Col Elwyn Righetti was never to be seen again by his compatriots after he crash-landed his flak-damaged P-51D following an attack on a Luftwaffe airfield on 17 April 1945.

Righetti had graduated as an Army Air Corps pilot on 26 July 1940 and then became involved in the training of new pilots. Despite his best efforts, it was not until October 1944 that he was finally released for combat. Righetti was assigned to the Eighth Air Force's 55th Fighter Group (FG) at Wormingford, in Essex, where he immediately began to make his presence felt. He shared in the destruction of a Bf 109 on 2 November 1944 and then downed two Focke-Wulf Fw 190s on Christmas Eve. Righetti destroyed another Bf 109 on 13 January 1945, and on 3 February intercepted some unusual adversaries – *Mistel* combinations comprising explosive-laden Junkers Ju 88s with Fw 190s attached to provide guidance to the target. Righetti quickly downed two *Mistels* to 'make ace', although his main reputation was as a successful ground strafer – once he found a Luftwaffe base full of aircraft he would have a field day.

By 17 April 1945, Righetti had been credited with 7.5 aerial and 18 strafing victories. That day he led his pilots down to attack Riesa/Canitz airfield, near Breslau, in Germany, where many Fw 190s and Bf 109s were spotted. Righetti's wingman, Capt Carroll Henry, reported that he had been instructed to attack a landing Fw 190 while his CO headed for the deck. Henry did as he was ordered, and as he pulled up and orbited the airfield, he saw a P-51 streaming coolant. It was Righetti's. He radioed, 'This is "Windsor". I'm hit bad, oil pressure dropping. I can't make it back. I have enough ammo for one more pass'.

Righetti made the pass, destroying an Fw 190, before crash-landing his Mustang. He then called, 'I broke my nose, but I'm okay. I got nine today. Tell my family I'm okay. It has been swell working with you gang' (*Cover artwork by Iain Wyllie*)

First published in Great Britain in 2003 by Osprey Publishing, Midland House, West Way, Botley, Oxford OX2 0PH, UK
443 Park Avenue South, New York, NY 10016, USA

ISBN 978 1 84176 437 5

Edited by Tony Holmes and Bruce Hales-Dutton
Page design by Tony Truscott
Cover Artwork by Iain Wyllie
Aircraft Profiles by Chris Davey
Photo Captions by Roger Freeman, William N Hess and Tony Holmes
Index by Alan Thatcher
Origination by Grasmere Digital Imaging, Leeds UK
Printed and bound in China through Bookbuilders
Typeset in Adobe Garamond and Univers

08 09 10 11 12   11 10 9 8 7 6 5 4 3 2

ACKNOWLEDGEMENTS
The Editor wishes to thanks Graham Cross, Roger Freeman, Dick Martin, Jerry Scutts, Sam Sox and John Stanaway for the provision of a number of the photographs which appear in this volume. All photographs reproduced in this book which lack a credit are via the author.

EDITOR'S NOTE
To make this best-selling series as authoritative as possible, the Editor would be interested in hearing from any individual who may have relevant photographs, documentation or first-hand experiences relating to the world's elite pilots, and their aircraft, of the various theatres of war. Any material used will be credited to its original source. Please write to Tony Holmes at 16 Sandilands, Chipstead, Sevenoaks, Kent, TN13 2SP, Great Britain, or by e-mail at: tony.holmes@zen.co.uk

For a catalogue of all Osprey Publishing titles please contact us at:

NORTH AMERICA
Osprey Direct, C/o Random House Distribution Center, 400 Hahn Road, Westminster, MD 21157
E-mail: **info@ospreydirect.com**

ALL OTHER REGIONS
Osprey Direct UK, P.O. Box 140, Wellingborough, Northants, NN8 2FA, UK
E-mail: **info@ospreydirect.co.uk**

CONTENTS

EDITOR'S INTRODUCTION

This volume is published as a companion to *Osprey Aircraft of the Aces 31 – VIII Fighter Command at War 'Long Reach'*, which had at its heart the training manual compiled by battle-seasoned USAAF fighter pilots for tyro aviators arriving fresh in the European Theatre of Operations (ETO) in 1944-45.

The Eighth Air Force was unique in bestowing ace status on pilots for ground kills, senior officers within VIII Fighter Command stating that there was more risk involved in strafing German aircraft on the ground than intercepting them in the air during the final year of the war in Europe. There is an element of truth in this, as far more aces were lost to flak than to Luftwaffe fighters during the Eighth Air Force's successful campaign in the ETO.

Bravery and skill were required to attack the numerous German airfields scattered across Europe, as these were heavily defended by flak batteries. In an attempt to reduce the haemorrhaging of VIII Fighter Command pilots in the summer of 1944, the command commissioned the compilation of a practical manual along the same lines at *'Long Reach'*. Contributions were made by all the leading strafing aces of the time, as well as group and squadron commanders. Entitled *'Down to Earth'*, the end product was a document written by combat veterans for future frontline pilots.

A significant chunk of the manual is reproduced in the second half of this Osprey volume. The remainder of the book charts the careers of the various strafing aces, and details a number of the more successful missions flown by the P-38, P-47 and P-51 squadrons assigned to VIII Fighter Command in 1944-45. Adding a dimension of colour to the work is the nine-page profile section by Chris Davey – all bar four of these artworks are brand new. Finally, over 130 black and white photographs sourced from private collections both in the USA and the UK make this volume a profusely illustrated addition to the *Aircraft of the Aces* series.

Tony Holmes
Sevenoaks, Kent
January 2003

PERIOD PREFACE 'DOWN TO EARTH'

Brigadier General FRANCIS H GRISWOLD
Chief of Staff VIII Fighter Command

The first priority job of our groups is escort of the Fortress and Liberator heavy bombers. It is long range, five...six...seven...hour stuff, to Berlin and back, to Poland and back, to Russia, and all of it at high altitude. Yet on 12 August 1944, at the height of the Battle of France, these same groups flew 46 missions comprising 1326 sorties as part of the greatest *ground* attack on record. Blanketing German supply lines north and north-east of Paris, our pilots bombed, burned and riddled with 0.50-cal armour-piercing incendiary 2616 railroad cars, 359 locomotives, 112 ammunition cars, 464 trucks, 362 oil cars, 9 oil tanks, 9 oil barges, 306 vehicles,

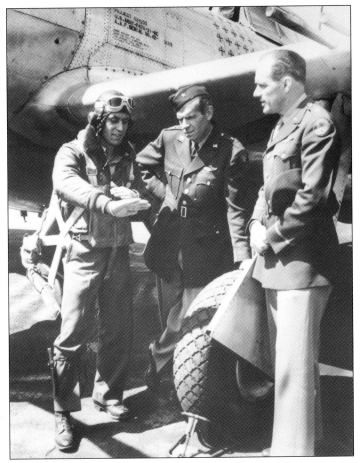

Brig Gen Francis Griswold (right), Chief of Staff VIII Fighter Command, and Brig Gen Jesse Auton, 65th Fighter Wing CO, listen intently to 56th FG 27-kill ace Robert S Johnson at Halesworth in 1944. The Eighth Air Force's 'top brass' were always interested in knowing what actual air combat was like for the crews within their command (*via Jerry Scutts*)

Maj Leroy Schreiber, CO of the 62nd FS, was one of the most popular and promising pilots in the 56th FG, claiming 12 aerial victories, 1 probable, six damaged and two destroyed on the ground between 30 July 1943 and 9 April 1944. He lost his life on 15 April 1944 when his P-47D (43-25577) was shot down by ground fire while strafing Flensburg airfield (*via Roger Freeman*)

15 bridges, 7 roundhouses, 13 buildings, 4 water towers, 19 aircraft, and many other targets. It was a big day, but not unique. On 13th, it was duplicated, and since the first part of March this year, VIII Fighter Command has, in this striking manner, been burning the enemy's deck.

The privilege of ground attack by fighters, if an operation so difficult can be called a privilege, must be won in the air by defeat of the enemy's air forces. This defeat in a long series of culminating battles in which this Command played a decisive part has been described in 'The Long Reach', and is already a part of the rapidly unfolding history of our Air Forces. Immediately our fighters pursued the grounded Luftwaffe to its airdromes, and there crippled it beyond hope of significant recovery.

Not only were our bomber missions freed from more than sporadic attack by this victory, but the enemy's entire transportation system was forced to depend for its defence upon flak and machine gun fire from the ground. Severe as this has been, and despite the losses we have suffered from it, this defence has never been enough to deter our fighters in their determined attack. Enemy locomotives, freight trains, troop trains, truck convoys, barges, oil tanks, ammunition dumps, coastal vessels, power houses, bridges, staff cars and communications have been victim of a hitherto unimaginable and unparalleled fighter ground assault across the entire face of Western Europe.

To the Command's achievement of 4009 enemy aircraft destroyed, 283 probably destroyed and 1339 damaged can now be added the destruction and serious damaging of rail and road transport by the thousands of locomotives, railroad cars and trucks on such a fantastic scale that to put it into figures fails to paint the picture. The real meaning is that from long before D-Day, and through it to the present, German supply and reinforcement has been destroyed or impeded to a point incompatible with the support of modern armies.

Since the beginning of this war the profit and loss on the proposition of fighter aircraft attacking ground targets has been the subject of professional debate and pilot discussion. Small profit to shoot up two or three trucks or a couple of machine guns for the loss of a valuable aircraft and pilot. Worse still when two . . . three . . . four go down over one well dispersed enemy airfield or, as on the days of our large scale attacks by the whole Command, 25 or more may be missing in action.

In addition to the loss of these aeroplanes and pilots is the unfortunate fact that our best, our outstanding leaders and fighters who had yet to meet their match in any enemy they could see, have gone down before the hidden gunfire or light flak associated with ground attack. Men such as Duncan, Beeson, Beckham, Gerald Johnson, Gabreski, Juchheim, Andrew, Hofer, Goodson, Schreiber, Millikan, Carpenter . . . the list could go on. For equal numbers engaged, four times as many pilots of this Command are lost on ground attack as in aerial combat. Light flak will ring an airfield, or a marshalling yard. Flak cars will open up in the middle of a train. A truck convoy, with sufficient warning, may be a hornet's nest. Every target of special value to the enemy will be heavily defended, and may exact its price.

Where then is the profit? The answer is the successful invasion and the victorious Battle of France. The answer is our flight of many a heavy bomber mission without challenge by enemy fighters, and the presence of our hordes of bombers and fighter-bombers over our troops in Normandy. The roads of France, strewn with enemy wreckage, reply, and an enemy starving for oil, ammunition, supplies, reinforcement could answer with deep feeling. The loss of every single one of our pilots is an individual and personal loss to us, but the harsh voice of war says clearly that had the entire VIII Fighter Command been wiped out in the course of its tremendous ground attack, the cost would have been well spent towards the purchase of mankind's victory.

In an all out war such as this, a successful air operation must pay the most and must cost the least. With fighter ground attack, as with other operations, experience has taught many lessons leading to this desirable end.

It is hoped that this bitterly gained experience may not be the only possible teacher, and that the recording of it in such publications as this, added to the instruction by those who have been through it, will point the way for replacements and new groups in this and other theatres, for pilots in training, and for those pilots and leaders of experience who have yet to encounter this special type of fighter duty. Like 'The Long Reach', 'Down to Earth' is a message from the battle at its height, told in their own words by the men who fight.

FRANCIS H GRISWOLD
Brigadier General, Commanding
VIII Fighter Command
September 1944

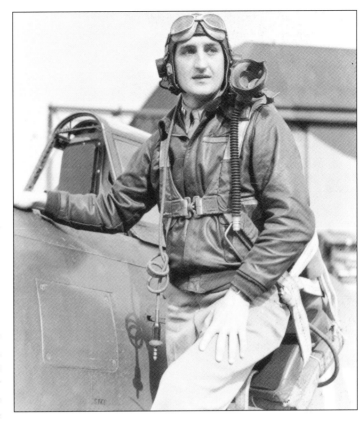

Capt 'Gabby' Gabreski strikes a fighter pilot's pose alongside the cockpit of a 61st FS/56th FG P-47C at Horsham St Faith in May 1943. He had yet to claim his first victory when this press photograph was taken. Like Schreiber, Gabreski would ultimately be lost whilst ground strafing (*via Sam Sox*)

ON TO THE OFFENSIVE

Maj Gen William E Kepner firmly believed in taking the offensive, but it was to be several months after he took over VIII Fighter Command in August 1943 that he was able to put his principles into practice because of a shortage of aircraft.

It was when Maj Gen James Doolittle assumed control of the Eighth Air Force in January 1944 that the command's mission changed significantly. Where it had previously been instructed to exclusively protect the bombers, VIII Fighter Command's fighters were now instructed to simply destroy the Luftwaffe at every opportunity.

Allied leaders meeting in Cairo in November 1943 had decided that the invasion of Europe should be scheduled for 1944. This meant establishing air superiority, but this could not be accomplished by ordering the fighters to remain with the bombers for the duration of their long escort missions. By the end of January 1944, therefore, the Eighth Air Force had abandoned 'close support' of the bombers in favour of 'ultimate pursuit', which allowed the fighters to follow the enemy until he was destroyed in the air or on the ground.

The fighters had often swept the skies ahead of the bomber stream and were allowed to engage the defending Luftwaffe. When the bombers were not under immediate threat, the escorting fighters were able to attack targets of opportunity on the ground. Indeed, several times in early 1944 returning USAAF P-47 Thunderbolt pilots claimed the destruction of enemy aircraft on the ground after strafing their airfields whilst flying back over occupied France, Belgium and Holland.

On 8 February 1944, a field order included a directive to VIII Fighter Command, which stated;

'If bombers are not being attacked, groups will detach one or two squadrons to range out searching for enemy aircraft. Upon withdrawal, if endurance permits, groups will search for and destroy enemy aircraft in the air and on the ground.'

In an effort to encourage pilots, the command also directed that enemy aircraft on the ground would count the same as those destroyed in the air. This edict, no doubt, caused many pilots who might not have been so eager for air-to-air combat to seek out ground targets whose destruction would enable them to become fighter aces in the Eighth Air Force.

Most, though, did not realise how well protected the Luftwaffe's airfields were, with numerous 20 mm and 40 mm guns supplementing armoured flak towers on major bases. By the end of the war these weapons would account for many more Eighth Air Force pilots than air-to-air combat. Indeed, most of the top air combat aces who were lost in 1944-45 were to fall to flak batteries.

The 353rd FG learned this lesson the hard way on 22 February 1944 when it was assigned escort duty for 177 B-24s of the 2nd Bomb Division. The fighters rendezvoused with the bombers and, because of the scale of the opposition, Lt Col Glenn E Duncan took his charges on wide sweeps in the vicinity of Bonn. North-east of the city he sighted an airfield on which a number of twin-engined aircraft were taxiing, with others parked on the perimeter. Duncan shot up a Ju 88, and as he pulled up to avoid heavy flak, he sighted two locomotives, which he also attacked.

As Duncan pulled up, other Thunderbolts came down to attack. One flight was led by Maj Walter Beckham, then the Eighth's leading ace with 18 aerial victories to his credit. Beckham picked out a line of six enemy aircraft and came in on a low-level firing pass at 425 mph. As he pulled up his P-47D (42-75226) was hit by flak and its engine was set on fire. Just before he baled out, Beckham called his wingman, 'Take the boys home, George, I can't make it'. He spent the rest of the war in captivity.

Early March 1944 brought the first bombing missions to Berlin. Some of the fiercest air battles of the war were fought between the Eighth and the Luftwaffe on the 6th and 8th of that month. Yet unbelievably, the third mission to the Reich's capital was unopposed. At this point, Gen Doolittle declared that the Luftwaffe had lost air superiority over Europe.

Following the Berlin mission, a spell of bad weather set in. This meant that that bombers could not fly because at that stage of the war they had no radar bombing capability. It also meant no missions for the fighter pilots. With the success of the strafing attack of 22 February, Duncan decided to go after the Luftwaffe on the ground. His philosophy was if they won't come up, or have no need to if the bombers aren't flying, why not go in on the deck and get them on their airfields? He therefore decided to see if VIII Fighter Command would be interested in forming a specialist ground strafing squadron. Kepner gave his approval and Duncan began recruiting immediately.

Sixteen pilots were signed up, namely 1Lts Kenneth Chetwood, Charles Durant, Francis Edwards and John A Sullivan from the 353rd FG, Capt Charles Ettlesen, 1Lts Clifford E Carter and Robert L Thacker and 2Lt John W Oliphint from the 359th FG, 1Lts Eugene W Kinnard, Martin H Johnson and Joseph Kelly from the 361st FG and

Seen here whilst still a captain, which dates this photograph as pre-December 1943, Walt Beckham had completed a tour in the Panama Canal Zone prior to joining the 353rd FG. He achieved 'acedom' on 10 October when he destroyed two Bf 110s and an 'Me 210' (almost certainly an Me 410) near Munster, and was made CO of the 351st FS the following month. Had Beckham not been downed by flak whilst strafing an airfield near Bonn on 22 February 1944, it is likely that he would have been the first ace in the ETO – if not the whole USAAF – to have passed Eddie Rickenbacker's 26-kill mark set in 1918. Beckham's combat record was truly impressive, for he downed 18 German fighters in just 57 missions. Reticent and small in physical stature, he was the top ace of the Eighth Air Force when brought down. His loss was the primary reason why fighter group commanders disliked sending their pilots on ground strafing missions. More aces were lost during such attacks than in combat in the air (*via Sam Sox*)

A member of 'Bill's Buzz Boys', Capt Norman J 'Bud' Fortier was one of the original 354th FS pilots sent to the ETO in July 1943. In two combat tours with the 355th FG, he flew 112 combat missions and cost the enemy five aircraft on the ground, plus one shared, as well as 5.833 in the air

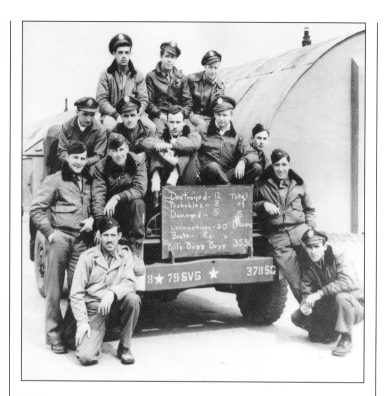

This is the nucleus of 'Bill's Buzz Boys', a team of fighter pilots from four different fighter groups who learned strafing tactics from Lt Col Glenn Duncan of the 353rd FG during the spring of 1944. Based at the 353rd FG's Metfield home, the men flew eight successful missions (83 effective sorties) together before returning to their units. The team's title recognised that it was VIII Fighter Command CO Gen William Kepner who had authorised their activities

Texan Col Glenn Duncan, CO of the 353rd FG, confers with his crew chief about the status of his P-47D *Dove of Peace*. Duncan set a shining example to his pilots, having achieved 19.5 aerial victories and 6.833 strafing kills prior to being shot down on 7 July 1944. Flying a series of fighters named the *Dove of Peace*, Duncan claimed all of his victories in the Thunderbolt. Like most US aces downed in the ETO, Duncan was 'bagged' by flak whilst strafing an airfield – this time it was Wesendorf, and the colonel force-landed his P-47D (42-25971) near Nienburg. Evading capture, Duncan made it to Holland, where he joined the Dutch resistance. He eventually returned to the 353rd FG in April 1945

Glenn Emile Duncan

Glenn Duncan was born on 19 May 1918 at Bering, Texas. He entered the Army Air Corps in 1940 and graduated from flying school at Kelly Field, Texas, on 4 October 1940.

Duncan built up considerable fighter experience before joining the 353rd FG in March 1943 as group operations officer – he was promoted to major in June 1943. The P-47-equipped 353rd FG arrived in England in June 1943, and Duncan scored his first aerial victory on 23 September 1943. He was promoted to lieutenant colonel in November 1943 and given command of the 353rd FG. Duncan continued his winning ways in the air against the Luftwaffe, and when D-Day approached he led his P-47s on numerous ground attack missions.

Duncan was one of the Eighth Air Force's top aces when he was downed by flak on 7 July 1944. He baled out and joined the Dutch underground, operating with it until April 1945. Once Holland was liberated he returned to England and took command of the 353rd FG once again.

After the war, Duncan stayed in the air force with the rank of colonel and served in numerous fighter command and staff positions until his retirement in February 1970.

His final score was 19.5 victories in the air and 6.833 on the ground.

Col Glenn E Duncan poses with his groundcrew as he runs up the engine of P-47D 42-25506 at a rather soggy Raydon in the early spring of 1944. This aircraft was the very first 'silver' Thunderbolt received by the 353th FG, and it was replaced by the identically-marked 42-25971 following a forced landing on 27 April 1944. The 350th FS's Lt Carl W Mueller was flying 42-25506 when it had to be bellied in at Copdock, near Ipswich, after suffering engine trouble minutes after taking off on a fighter-bomber mission that was bound for France. The P-47 was salvaged, rather than repaired. As the sixth LH-X flown by Duncan, 42-25506 was distinguished by the application of a small Roman VI alongside the X (*via Michael O'Leary*)

Capt Albert B Starr, 1Lts Norman J Fortier and Kenneth B Williams and 2Lt Gilbert S Wright from the 355th FG . In honour of Gen Kepner, they named themselves 'Bill's Buzz Boys'.

After training, the unit flew its first mission on 26 March 1944 when Duncan led a formation of 12 P-47s – four of which carried fragmentation bombs – on a sweep of northern France. They attacked airfields at Chartres, Chateaudun, Anaet, St-André-de-l'Eure and Beauvais, claiming one twin-engined aircraft destroyed, one probably destroyed and four damaged. Additionally, a hangar, a flak tower and a water tower were strafed and various small buildings damaged.

Duncan's most successful mission came three days later, again against airfields in France. His pilots claimed seven enemy aircraft destroyed, five probably destroyed and five damaged, plus eight locomotives and a hangar destroyed and numerous other targets damaged.

A mission against an airfield in north-west Germany on 1 April accounted for three Ju 88s destroyed on the ground and 13 locomotives badly damaged. The final mission for 'Bill's Buzz Boys' came just 11 days later, when the outfit destroyed seven locomotives and set two railway wagons on fire in north-west Germany.

Two of the 4th FG's leading aces pose for an official USAAF photograph at Debden in early March 1944. Duane Beeson (left) finished the war with 17.333 aerial and 4.75 strafing kills and Don Gentile (right) was credited with 21.833 aircraft destroyed in the air and six on the ground. Both men subsequently died in the immediate post-war years, Beeson of a brain tumour in 1947 and Gentile in a flying accident in 1951 (*via Michael O'Leary*)

Flying a total of eight missions, the special unit destroyed 14 aircraft, probably destroyed six and damaged 14 on the ground. It also strafed 17 locomotives, one boat, one hangar and nine flak towers. Two pilots were lost and 13 P-47s damaged.

On 12 April the following message arrived from Gen Kepner;

'Upon completion of today's mission the flying unit known as "Bill's Buzz Boys" will be dissolved and pilots and aeroplanes returned to their proper stations. The commanding general expresses his sin-

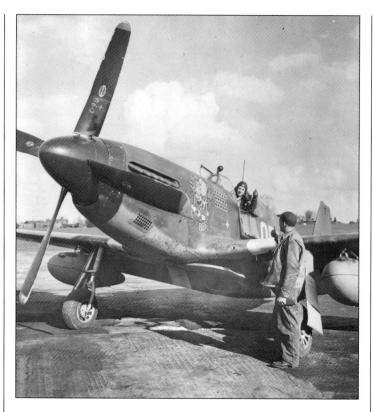

Duane Beeson's *BEE*, alias P-51B 43-6819 QP-B of the 334th FS/4th FG, was photographed at Debden on 12 April 1944. The white cross near the wing root indicates that the aircraft has had a fuselage tank installed. Claiming 4.75 strafing kills, Beeson achieved all of these in this very aircraft. He was also shot down in 43-6819 while attacking an airfield near Brandenburg-Briest on 5 April 1944 (*via Roger Freeman*)

cere appreciation to each pilot, and to those supervisory personnel, contributing to the successful development of new fighter tactics.'

Other units were also beginning to strafe targets as well, with the P-51B-equipped 4th FG achieving success on 27 March. After escorting bombers to Cazaux airfield in France, pilots observed a number of enemy aircraft still undamaged after the raid. Maj James Clark ordered the 334th and 336th FSs to attack them, and Capt Duane W Beeson immediately set a Ju 88 on fire and, on the opposite side of the field, hit a Henschel Hs 126, which immediately blew up. Beeson subsequently reported;

'I made a pass at a Ju 88 and observed strikes all along the fuselage, and then attacked a Ju 88 whose port engine burst into flames. After we had broken away from the aero-drome and were climbing above it, I saw an aircraft enveloped in flames and a couple of minor explosions as though the gas tanks had ignited. I believe this attack was successful for our squadron because we were able to hit the aerodrome right after the heavy bombers had left, decreasing the danger from light flak until our attack was finished.'

Beeson was credited with the destruction of a Ju 88 and a Hs 126, and with damaging a second Ju 88.

They always said tall boys could not fit in fighters but, at 6 ft 4 ins, Capt James N McElroy proved not only that it was possible, but that it could be done very successfully. McElroy, who flew a Mustang with the 358th FS/355th FG, scored five times in the air and destroyed another six enemy aircraft on the ground. Five of the latter (all Do 217s) were claimed by McElroy during an attack on Glienicke airfield on 15 April 1944

One of five pilots within the 355th FG to score ten or more strafing kills, Lt Ray 'Silky' Morris of the 354th FS saw combat in the ETO from October 1943 through to July 1944, when he completed his 74-mission tour. During that time he claimed 3.5 aerial and ten strafing kills, all with the P-51B. Seen here with his groundcrew towards the end of his tour, Morris is sitting in the cockpit of his assigned P-51B 42-106437 *Darlin' Dorris*

Capt Albert Schlegel was one of the 4th FG's many RAF-trained pilots, and he scored his first victory on 2 October 1943 while flying a P-47. But it was as a Mustang pilot that he hit his stride, downing eight Luftwaffe aircraft and sharing the destruction of a ninth, in addition to the five he destroyed on the ground. Schlegel met the same fate as many other VIII Fighter Command pilots when he was shot down and killed by flak near Strasbourg on 28 August 1944. He was one of five 4th FG pilots lost to flak on this day, three of whom were killed

Lt Hipolitus 'Tom' Biel is a relatively unknown ace from the 334th FS/4th FG. He downed his first kill on 4 January 1944, and had built his score up to 5.3 aerial victories and six destroyed on the ground by the time he was killed in combat with enemy fighters on 24 April 1944

He also shared credit for destroying a third Ju 88. Altogether, the two squadrons claimed 23 enemy aircraft destroyed on the ground. The price was one of its veteran pilots, Capt Archie Chatterly, who was hit by flak and baled out to become a prisoner of war.

The following day the 355th FG visited the airfield at Dijon, where Maj Edward Szaniawski led the 357th FS down to destroy 19 enemy aircraft. Szaniawski topped the scoring with 3.67 kills, while pilots from the group's remaining two squadrons chalked up another five to make a total of 23.67 for the day.

A massive 11-group low-level attack on against German airfields was ordered by VIII Fighter Command on 5 April, although the weather was so bad that only three units were able to participate. Of this trio, the 4th and 355th FGs had assignments deep in the Munich area, and they turned in remarkable performances.

Despite the weather, Lt Col William Cummings was able to get below the overcast and attack the targeted airfields south-west of the city. Opposed by heavy ground fire, the attack lasted 40 minutes, and left 43 enemy aircraft destroyed on the ground and at least 80 more damaged.

Another eight were shot down. Three Mustangs were lost, two of them to ground fire. For this outstanding performance, the 355th FG was awarded a Distinguished Unit Citation.

The 4th FG also had a good day on 5 April when it attacked enemy airfields in the same area. Two kills were scored in the air, while the P-51 pilots destroyed 47 enemy aircraft on the ground. Maj James Goodson reported;

'I told the squadron that the aerodrome (Stendal) was at "ten o'clock" and we went in for the attack from north-east to south-

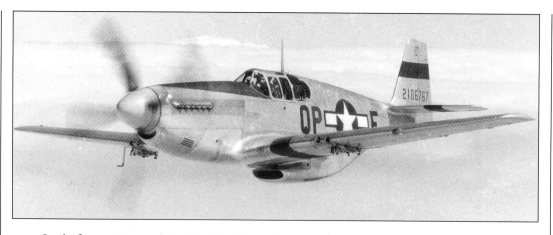

west. On the first pass I covered a Ju 52 with strikes and then moved my sights on to an Fw 190. I would not have claimed the '190, but Lt Carlson – my No 3 – says that I set it on fire. I pulled up and watched the others sweep across. I saw that about ten enemy aircraft were burning, and that there was no flak, so I ordered another pass and lined up on three Ju 88s parked wing tip-to wing-tip on the south-west corner. As I passed over, two were blazing but at least one was shared with Lt Emerson.

'I then attacked a Ju 88 in front of the north hangar and pulled up to see it burning. Capt Gentile and I then destroyed another Ju 88 on a hard stand on the northern extension – I was able to pull up and see that these two Ju 88s were burning nicely. I then circled the 'drome taking pictures of the three Ju 88s which were wing-tip to wing-tip, and saw them blazing fiercely. As I watched, the end one collapsed and fell apart. As I circled, 25 aircraft were blazing, including my original two with the '190. We left because we were out of ammunition, and the aerodrome was almost obscured by huge columns of smoke.'

Since its combat initiation in late November 1943, the 20th FG had been handicapped by the performance of its Lockheed P-38s. The fighter's twin Allison engines were not designed for the cold and damp-ness of northern Europe and, to make matters worse, the cockpit heating system was also inadequate for the theatre. Although pilots wore the warmest clothing they could find, it was never enough. Literally bundled up in layers of clothing, they found it difficult to manoeuvre their aircraft effectively in combat. However, with the improvement of the weather in the spring of 1944, the group's combat effectiveness also increased.

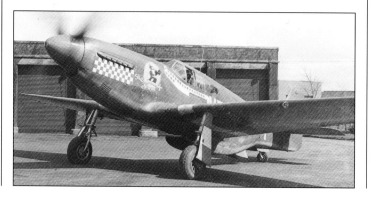

Herbert Blanchfield of the 4th FG's 334th FS claimed 4.333 strafing kills within weeks of receiving this P-51B in the early spring of 1944. His successful run came to an abrupt end on the morning of 9 May 1944 when he was shot down in this very aircraft whilst strafing a flak tower during an attack on St Dizier airfield. Blanchfield spent the rest of the war as a PoW (*via Roger Freeman*)

Capt Don Gentile's flamboyantly decorated P-51B 43-6913 VF-T of the 336th FS/4th FG. Named *Shangri-La*, it carried a block of red and white checkerboard on both sides of the nose below the exhaust manifold. John Godfrey, who often flew as Gentile's wingman, had a similar marking applied to his P-51B. The purpose of this duplication was, allegedly, so that both pilots could easily identify the other's aircraft during the heat of battle. Surprisingly, this embellishment was tolerated by higher command. Gentile was one of the first strafing aces, although most, it not all, of his six ground kills may have been scored in P-51B 43-6572 (*via Roger Freeman*)

Col Harold Rau, CO of the 20th FG, poses with his crew, T/Sgt James A Douglas, Sgt Grant L Beach and S/Sgt Luther W Ghent at Kings Cliffe in May 1944. Sitting at Rau's feet is his dog 'Honey'. Rau assumed command of the group on 20 March 1944, and he was in turn relieved by Lt Col Cy Wilson at the end of June. He then took charge again on 27 August following the loss of his successor over Germany (Wilson was made a PoW). Rau remained CO until 18 December, when he came to the end of his extended tour in the ETO. Fitted with external tanks, the CO's P-38J has had its nose cone polished in the hope that Luftwaffe pilots would think that the aircraft was an unarmed photo-recce Lightning. Harry Rau scored all five of his kills (one Bf 109G shot down and four twin-engined aircraft strafed) during a single mission on 8 April 1944. The colonel named all his personal aircraft *Gentle Annie*. P-38J-10 42-68165, coded MC-R, boasts five swastika victory markings, as well as a locomotive destroyed symbol forward of the swastikas. Originally in natural metal finish, this aircraft received an application of dark green to its uppersurfaces in accordance with VIII Fighter Command advice pending the launch of the cross-Channel invasion, and the likelihood of Eighth Air Force fighters moving to the continent (*via M O'Leary*)

On 20 March command of the 20th FG had been assumed by Lt Col Harold Rau, who was busily seeking a solution to his group's lack of activity during the poor weather when the bombers could not operate. He was to find the action he sought on 8 April, when the 20th was sent on a low level sweep over central Germany. Rau led the 79th FS to the airfield at Satzwedel, where a Heinkel He 177 bomber was caught in the landing pattern. A flight of P-38s fired together to send it crashing to earth. Two more He 177s also went down moments later, and three Ju 88s and two Ju 52/3m transports were set ablaze on the ground. All were destroyed on the first pass. Before the attack was over the 79th had accounted for another pair of Ju 88s and a He 111.

As the squadron departed, it spotted a target of opportunity. Some 300 German infantrymen were marching along a road, and the resulting strafing passes no doubt accounted for a good number of them. As the 79th FS broke off its attack, Col Rau came upon two supply trains moving parallel to each other in opposite directions. He instructed Maj R C Franklin to take the south-bound train while he took the north-bound one. As the trains moved close to each other, the two P-38 pilots bored in and opened fire. The boilers of each locomotive exploded and the trains came to a halt, streaming plumes of white steam.

Then the 79th encountered a flight of seven Bf 109s. One of the Lightnings was hit immediately, although the pilot was able to bale out. Lt Col Rau latched onto the tail of one of the fighters and sprayed it with cannon strikes, but as the enemy pilot tried to escape, he rammed the tail of the P-38 flown by 26-mission veteran Lt Mitchell P Snow and both aircraft went down in flames. Snow, who had claimed a Bf 109 destroyed just minutes earlier, was killed. As the fight continued two more Bf 109s were destroyed before the rest broke off.

The 77th FS, meanwhile, had encountered a gaggle of German bombers about to land. The Lightnings struck from 200 ft and raked the enemy aircraft on the ground, making several passes. Eight bombers were left in flames, with another 20 or so badly damaged. One P-38 was lost to ground fire, but moments later Lt Claude Home encountered an Fw 190 which he pursued and it exploded.

Low on fuel, the 77th FS headed for home, but they had not finished. En route, Capt Dick Morris attacked a locomotive pulling tanker wagons loaded with fuel. He fired a long burst, the engine exploded and the trucks blossomed heavy red flames one after another.

Pilots of the 55th FS also attacked trains during the mission, destroying eight locomotives and leaving three large oil dumps spewing black columns of smoke in Ulzen area. As the P-38s headed for home, they expended the balance of their ammunition on assorted buildings, bridges and any other targets that presented themselves.

P-38J-10 42-67717 was the personal mount of leading Eighth Air Force P-38 ace James 'Slick' Morris of the 20th FG's 77th FS. Aside from his 7.333 aerial kills, Morris also claimed 2.833 strafing victories (*via Sam Sox*)

When the 20th returned to Kings Cliffe, its pilots were able to celebrate becoming part of a potent low level destruction machine. They were credited with destroying or badly damaging 18 locomotives, 50 freight or oil tanker trucks, two bridges, 16 flak towers and gun positions and 50 aircraft. They had expended 4000 20 mm cannon shells and 22,000 rounds of 0.50-cal ammunition. The group, which was to become known as VIII Fighter Command's 'loco busters', had now realised the destructive power of the 20 mm cannon and four 0.50-cal machine guns mounted in the nose of their aircraft.

The 355th FG's 357th FS also enjoyed success on 8 April when it attacked Gifhorn airfield. Seven aircraft were destroyed on the ground and a Bf 109 shot down. Three pilots were killed during the course of this mission, however, one of whom was the 355th FS's first ace, Capt Norman Olson – he fell victim to flak near Celle in P-51B 43-6589.

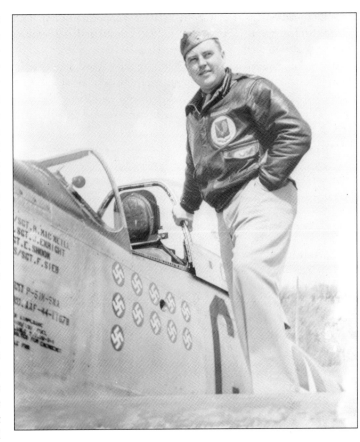

Irwin H Dregne served with the 357th FG in its early days of combat and returned to become its last commander in December 1944. He flew Mustangs displaying the name *Bobby Jeanne* on the left hand side and *Ah Fung Goo* on the right. His final score was five kills in the air and 5.5 on the ground

Two days later the 4th FG's Maj James Goodson led the 336th FS against the Luftwaffe airfield at Romorantin, in France, where a lot of training aircraft were caught on the ground. He subsequently reported;

'I made half a dozen passes at Hs 126s and other trainers. I obtained good strikes on six different enemy aircraft and made sure that all six were left blazing, but it is possible that at least two were shared with Lt Shilke or some other pilot. I left the aerodrome when I could find no aircraft left to attack. As I left, the main hangar went up in an enormous pall of smoke reaching to 8000 ft, and visible from the French coast. Some 20+ aircraft were burning. I claimed four enemy aircraft destroyed on the ground and two shared.'

There was major action both in the air and on the ground for VIII Fighter Command on 11 April. The partially P-51-equipped 352nd FG escorted B-17s to their targets and then dived to attack enemy airfields on the way home. The 486th FS hit Stendal, where it destroyed five aircraft on the ground and shot down two, and the 487th FS swooped on two airfields in the Berlin area and made repeated passes, destroying 13 aircraft and damaging three more. Lt Carl Luksic led the way with four and three damaged. He also shot up a locomotive on the way home. The group's overall score was 20 aircraft destroyed for the loss of one Mustang.

The 355th FG also had a good day. During a mission to Sorau, the unit encountered a large gaggle of twin-engined aircraft attacking the bombers. The group shot down nine before the Bf 109s and Fw 190s

James Alexander Goodson

James Goodson was born on 21 March 1921 in New York. He had studied in Europe and was aboard the SS *Athena* en route to the USA when it was torpedoed on 3 September 1939. Goodson returned to England, where he joined the RAF and, following training as a fighter pilot, was assigned to No 133 'Eagle' Sqn.

He transferred to the United States Army Air Force in September 1942 and joined the 336th FS. Goodson scored his first air-to-air victory on 22 June 1943 while flying a P-47 Thunderbolt. He added two more on 16 August, becoming an ace on 7 January 1944, by which time he held the rank of captain.

In March 1944 Goodson was promoted to major and given command of the 336th FS. He continued to score aerial victories after his unit was issued with P-51 Mustangs, and on 21 March he began destroying enemy aircraft on the ground.

On a fighter sweep to Romorantin aerodrome in France Goodson was credited with the destruction of five enemy aircraft on the ground, with a sixth shared. During the spring of 1944, Goodson's score both in the air and on the ground continued to grow, and he duly became one of the Eighth Air Force's top aces. However, his P-51 fell to flak on 20 June 1944 when he was strafing Neubrandenburg aerodrome, and Goodson spent the rest of the war as a PoW.

He left the service at the end of the war to enter the business world. After heading several companies in Europe, Goodson became vice president of International Telephone and Telegraph Corporation. Now in retirement, Goodson lives in England. His final tally was 14 enemy aircraft destroyed in the air and 15 on the ground.

4th FG ace Maj James Goodson poses in P-51B 43-2484 VF-B, which features 30 black swastika symbols denoting both his air and ground strafing credits. This photograph was taken at Debden sometime after the ace claimed his final success on 25 May 1944. Goodson was officially credited with 14 aerial and 15 strafing victories. Therefore, the 30th swastika applied to the Mustang almost certainly signifies his solitary probable kill, which he claimed on 3 September 1943 (*via Roger Freeman*)

arrived. Following this action the 354th and 357th FSs worked over Strasbourg airfield, accounting for 14 more enemy aircraft.

The 356th FG got in on the ground strafing act that day too when the 361st FS claimed 13 aircraft destroyed at Gifhorn airfield. Lt Raymond Gansberg led the scoring with two Ju 88s and two Bf 110s. Two of the attacking aircraft fell to flak, however.

The 355th FG went back to Germany on 13 April, escorting bombers attacking airfields near Munich. On the way home the 354th and 357th FSs strafed Oberpaffenhofen and Grailsheim airfields, the 354th accounting for 19 aircraft destroyed. Maj Claiborne Kinnard was credited with the destruction of three Ju 88s and a Do 217, making him the most successful pilot involved in this action.

On 18 April the 352nd FG flew one of its first missions with the P-51 Mustang when the group's newly-converted 486th and 487th FSs provided top cover for the P-47s of the 328th FS, the latter unit in turn flying one of its final Thunderbolt missions. The P-47 pilots attacked the airfield at Quackenbruck, where they found more than 20 parked aircraft. Following the strafing passes, 12 were left as burning wrecks, with five others probably destroyed and two more damaged. Several buildings and storage facilities were also shot up.

A He 111 explodes in flame, this aircraft being one of three Heinkel bombers 56th FG CO 'Hub' Zemke destroyed during a strafing attack on the dispersal area at Husum on 15 April 1944 (*via Roger Freeman*)

There was a new mode of attack for the 356th FG on 23 April. This involved the 359th FS hitting Hagenau airfield first with fragmentation bombs, followed by the group's remaining two squadrons performing a series of dive-bombing attacks. Repeated strafing passes by all three squadrons then followed. The result was three aircraft destroyed and 27

Claiborne Kinnard was an outstanding presence within the 355th FG except for the few months when he commanded the 4th FG during the autumn of 1944. He returned to the 355th in February 1945 as its CO. During that year he destroyed 10.5 enemy aircraft on the ground, taking his total strafing tally to 17. He also enjoyed some aerial successes in the final weeks of the war in Europe, downing a pair of Bf 109s on 20 April 1945 to take his overall tally to eight

damaged, but the cost to the 356th was the loss of three aircraft to flak and their pilots captured. Amongst the latter was group CO, and 5.5-kill strafing ace, Col Einar Malmstrom (in P-47D 42-25513).

Many Luftwaffe fighters were encountered during long-range missions on 24 April, and after the aerial combat, numerous groups attacked the enemy in its own backyard. That day USAAF fighter pilots claimed 124 aircraft shot down, with 66 of these victories being achieved in the air. Amongst the most successful units was the 352nd FG's 486th FS, which attacked four enemy airfields. The headliner for the 24th was the 486th's Lt Edwin Heller, who set a new strafing record with seven victories. He reported;

'Blue Flight consisted of Capt Robert McKean and myself. We had permission to strafe a field in the approximate area of Ingolstadt, and we made a pass in from west to east. We each picked out a line of three aeroplanes. I was behind Capt McKean and saw his strikes on all three. We circled to the left on the deck and came back for a second pass, this time from north to south.

Claiborne Kinnard was the first combat commander of the 355th FG's 354th FS, which had a bulldog for its emblem. Naturally, numerous Mustangs flown by the unit carried the nickname *The Bulldogs* on their engine cowlings, although only this particular machine (P-51B 43-6431) bore the number 1, signifying its assignment to the CO. All of Kinnard's Mustangs were named *MAN o' WAR*, the titling being applied in white paint on an irregular shaped red backing. Kinnard used this particular P-51B to claim at least five of his seventeen strafing kills (*via Roger Freeman*)

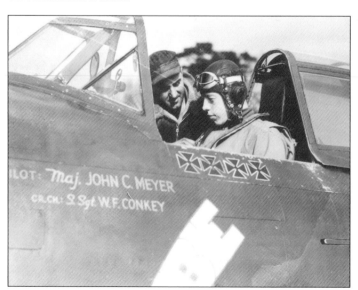

Maj John C 'Whips' Meyer is helped with his straps as he settles into the cockpit of *LAMBIE* (painted in white), alias P-47D 42-8529. Long-time CO of the 352nd FG's 487th FS, and later deputy group CO, Brooklyn-born Meyer claimed all four of his Thunderbolt (aerial) kills with this machine in November-December 1943. Note the thick panel of bullet-proof glass immediately ahead of the fighter's gunsight. Meyer proved to be successful both in aerial combat and in airfield raids, and had he not been severely injured in a car accident in January 1945 he might have been top scorer in the ETO. As it was, he ran up a total of 24 aerial and 13 strafing victories (*via Roger Freeman*)

P-51B 42-106471 was John Meyer's first Mustang, and he claimed 5.5 aerial victories with it in April-May 1944. The tally carried below the fighter's cockpit includes its pilot's kills in the P-47, as well as seven ground strafing victories in this very aircraft. *Lambie II* was lost on 7 June 1944 when it spun in over southern England after completing a strafing mission in support of the D-Day landings. It pilot, Lt Clifford Garney, was killed in the crash (*via Sam Sox*)

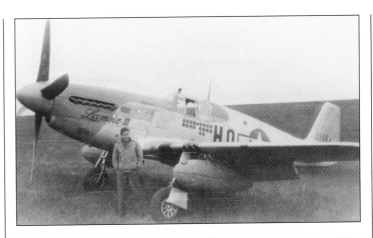

P-51D 44-14696 *HELL-ER-BUST* was the last Mustang assigned to Capt Ed Heller of the 486th FS. He flew two combat tours with the 352nd FG, becoming both an aerial and strafing ace. Heller twice destroyed seven enemy aircraft during attacks on German airfields, on 16 April 1944 and 24 April 1945. He returned to combat over Korea and was credited with destroying 3.5 MiG-15s prior to he himself being shot down and made a PoW in January 1953

'We each picked out two aeroplanes in the south-east corner of the field. I damaged one and destroyed the other. Capt McKean destroyed both of his. We then made a 180-degree turn on the deck, keeping low. I was still behind Capt McKean, and I saw him hit the ground in a ploughed field in a cloud of dust. He said over the radio he was hit and was going to bale out. He couldn't get the altitude, however, and decided to crash land. He was trying to make it to another field and I thought he was going to make it fine, when he suddenly dropped in from about 50 ft, just on the edge of the field. His aeroplane broke up and burst into flames. I circled it two or three times at 100 ft, but could not see him get out.'

Later information indicated that McKean had struck a high tension wire (in P-51B 43-7198) and was killed in the subsequent crash. Heller continued;

'I climbed to 10,000 ft and started home by myself. After about 15 minutes I saw an airfield with about 35+ aeroplanes on it. I circled it and planned my approach and picked out my targets. I hit the deck at about two miles from the field and approached the field on the tree-tops. As I

Lt Ed Heller's P-51B-5 43-6704 *HELL-ER-BUST* was photographed 'in the field' at Bodney on a sunny day in May 1944. The Mustang displays ten German crosses along its cowling, the bulk of these signifying strafing kills. Heller's fighter was one of the first Mustangs within the 352nd FG to be fitted with a 'blown' Malcolm hood, and this was due primarily to the pilot's height (*via Sam Sox*)

Maj Stephen W Andrew was a veteran of the Pacific theatre who also enjoyed combat success in the ETO flying with the 352nd FG's 486th FS. He was credited with eight aerial and 6.5 strafing kills before becoming a PoW on 2 July 1944 – his Mustang suffered mechanical failure over Hungary, forcing Andrew to belly land deep inside enemy territory

saw the field before me, I zoomed up 100 ft and came down on three Me 110s in a row. I could see strikes on the trio. I kept low across the field, and after I was away from it I zoomed up. I looked back and saw two aeroplanes smoking and in flames. I then climbed up to 10,000 ft and started home.

'After about ten minutes I saw another field. I repeated the same tactics and approached the field by a big hangar. I sprayed it and jumped over it. There was a mass of aeroplanes right in front of me. I hit three of them good, but I set only one of them on fire. I was out in the middle of the field then and saw an Me 110 at the end of the runway at a 45-degree angle from me. I skidded around right off the field and gave it a long burst and saw it burst into flames.

Capt Edwin L Heller joined the 352nd FG in December 1943 and achieved his first two kills – two Bf 109s – on 8 May 1944. He completed his first combat tour with 4.5 aerial victories, and eventually became an aerial ace on 2 March 1945 when he downed a Bf 109. Heller had completed 520 combat hours by VE-Day

Edwin Lewis Heller

Edwin Heller was born on 5 December 1918 in Philadelphia, Pennsylvania. He entered the Army Air Corps in May 1942 and graduated from pilot training on 15 February 1943. Heller joined the 352nd FG's 486th FS following graduation and went to England with the group. A late starter, Heller gained his first two aerial victories on 8 May 1944. He scored two more aerial victories and shared another before completing his first combat tour – he had also claimed 7.5 strafing kills.

Heller returned to the ETO in the autumn of 1944, becoming an aerial ace in March 1945 and taking his tally of strafing kills to 14.5 during the spring of 1945, with seven gained during a single mission. He was promoted to major before leaving the service in 1945. Heller later joined the air force, serving as a fighter pilot in Korea where he was credited with 3.5 MiG-15s destroyed before being shot down in January 1953 to become a PoW.

Heller had been promoted to lieutenant colonel shortly before he was shot down, and on his return from captivity he remained in the USAF until retirement in 1967. Heller's total score was 5.5 aerial victories and 14.5 on the ground in World War 2, followed by 3.5 aerial victories in Korea.

'I also killed one of the groundcrew who stood there and looked at me. When I looked at this field after I zoomed up, two of the aeroplanes were smoking and burning. I climbed up to 10,000 ft and proceeded home without any other excitement.'

Heller claimed a total of five Bf 110s and one unidentified enemy aircraft destroyed on the ground, plus a sixth Bf 110 damaged. Apparently, the damage claim was later upgraded to a confirmed victory, for Heller was credited with seven enemy aircraft destroyed on the ground. For his outstanding performance that day he was awarded the Distinguished Service Cross.

PRELUDE TO D-DAY

By mid-May 1944, the Eighth Air Force had realised it was time to switch from strategic to tactical operations in preparation for the Normandy landings scheduled for early June. It was therefore decided to turn the fighters loose on the enemy's ground transport.

Accordingly, on 21 May, VIII Fighter Command assigned each of its fighter groups a separate target for Operation *Chattanooga*. A total of 552 fighters – P-38s, P-47s and P-51s – descended on Europe like clouds of locusts to attack all forms of transportation. Hardest hit were railways and rolling stock. That day the fighters destroyed 91 locomotives and damaged another 134. Bridges and stations were attacked and left badly damaged, while many vehicles were destroyed on the roads.

The airfields were not neglected either, and over 100 aircraft felt the fury of the attacking American fighters. Maj John Lowell of the newly-arrived 364th FG led his Lightnings against airfields at Parchim, Ludwigslust and Hagenow. Lowell left three Ju 52/3ms and Ju 88s in flames after his firing passes, while the rest of his section accounted for another five aircraft.

The 55th FG led the field in destroyed locomotives for the day when they wrecked 23 and damaged another 15 while shooting up anything else they could find in the vicinity. The 339th FG did its dirty work between Dresden and Leipzig, destroying 14 aircraft in the air and another ten on the ground. The price was heavy, however, with the group losing four pilots and having a further six aircraft damaged. Lt Harold Everett was most fortunate to return as he pulled up from strafing a train and ran through some high-tension wires on his way out. He reported;

'I had to pull up and break off as I had about 300 ft of wire and cross-tie dangling off my left wing. I landed at Framlingham to get gas and inspect the damage, as the wing had begun to vibrate halfway home. The spinner was chewed up and the prop was damaged, plus the air scoop was flattened.'

The 352nd FG was also involved in heavy action, its 328th FS taking

Maj Michael J Jackson of the 62nd FS/56th FG achieved all of his successes – eight aerial and 5.5 strafing kills – between 4 July 1944 and 14 January 1945

the day's laurels by destroying 22 aircraft on the ground. Capt Earl Abbott led his flight to Altruppin airfield, which they dive-bombed before going down to strafe any surviving aircraft. The pilots destroyed an Fw 190 before the ground fire became too intense and they had to leave. The second field they attacked was less well defended, and ten aircraft were destroyed there. Capt Robert Sharp then brought his section down to destroy another 11 aircraft, thus matching Abbott's feat.

The following day, four groups were sent to attack bridges at Hasselt, in Belgium. The 78th and 356th FGs engaged in skip-bombing attacks while the 56th FG used dive-bombing tactics. On 23 May the heavy bombers targeted marshalling yards and airfields in France, and on this occasion the fighters left it to their 'big friends' to do the damage, returning to base without making any low-level attacks.

After this series of communications-wrecking missions, the fighters returned to long-range escort and were involved in a number of aerial combats. But it was just as important for the groups to preserve their strength in preparation for the landings because it was not known how much opposition the Luftwaffe could put up. It was crucial for VIII Fighter Command to maintain air superiority over the landing beaches and provide air cover for the ground forces while they established beachheads. At the last possible moment the now famous zebra stripes were applied to all participating aircraft.

D-Day, 6 June 1944, and every available VIII Fighter Command aircraft was airborne. Take-offs began as early as 0300 hrs and flying continued until after 2300 hrs. During the early morning most flights were conducted at between 8000 and 17,000 ft above the landing forces. Later in the day hundreds of Mustangs, Lightnings and Thunderbolts dropped down to carry out bombing and strafing missions.

Twenty-five fighters were lost during the day, nine of them from the 4th FG – the 334th FS lost a whole flight of four, led by Maj Winslow Sobanski, when it was caught at low level by 15 Fw 190s. Several of the 25 fighters were downed by flak and two were involved in a mid-air collision.

The 56th FG flew seven missions on D-Day. Following the two early morning sweeps to cover the landing force, the group began its tactical support programme on the third flight of the day with a dive-bombing attack on Les Andelys, followed by a glide bombing assault on Le Tréport.

The day's fifth mission, led by Capt Fred Christensen, was quite successful. His section carried out skip-bombing in the Rambouillet area, destroying an Fw 190 and hitting 20 trains, including a troop train, as well as four armoured cars, a petrol tanker, buses and four staff cars.

Lt Col Claiborne Kinnard led one of the seven missions flown by the 355th FG on D-Day. His aircraft caught railway wagons and ammunition trucks in the Le Mans area, and after bombing them, they dived down to strafe their targets. The explosions were spectacular – so much so that some P-51s returned with debris lodged in wings and fuselages.

The exploits of 353rd FG ace Capt James Poindexter provide a good picture of the missions flown after the invasion;

'I was leading "Jockey" (352nd FS) blue flight on a dive-bombing mission to Margny airfield at Compiègne, in France, on 7 June. Due to adverse weather conditions, we missed the target on the way in but pin-pointed the location at Soissons. I observed large concentrations of

Maj George L Merritt Jr was CO of the 375th FS/361st FG from 27 August 1943 until he was killed on 7 June 1944. Leading a fighter-bomber sweep near Nantes, some 125 miles south-west of the Allied beachhead, on D-Day+1, Merritt spotted a column of German vehicles and led his charges in at tree-top height against the enemy. His wingman, 2Lt Sherman Armsby, reported his demise upon returning to the group's Bottisham base. 'The pass was made over the woods, where Maj Merritt (in P-51B 42-106835) hit a post, skipped off the road and exploded. He landed upside down in a field in a ball of fire.' The most aggressive, and colourful, squadron CO in the 361st FG, Merritt had claimed three aerial kills flying P-47s and two in P-51s. Additionally, he was credited with the destruction of six aircraft on the ground (three apiece in the P-47 and P-51)

A good in flight shot of P-51D 44-13537 *SWEET THING IV*, flown by Lt Col Roy A Webb Jr, CO of the 374th FS/361st FG. Webb completed his tour in July 1944 with four aerial and five strafing victories. All of the latter (Fw 190s) were claimed on 29 June 1944 when the 361st attacked Oschersleben airfield in eastern Germany

Claiborne Kinnard's fourth *MAN O' WAR* whilst leading the 354th FS/355th FG was P-51D 44-15625, which featured 'in-the-field' camouflage on the fuselage upper decking. Like Kinnard's previous fighters with this name, the *MAN O' WAR* titling was painted in white on a red bulged shape backing (*via Roger Freeman*)

railcars and locomotives in the marshalling yard at this point, so jockeyed the flight into position for a run from 5000 ft against this target. Six of the eight 500-lb bombs dropped scored direct hits in a concentrated area of 50+ rail vehicles. After the blast and smoke had cleared, I observed wreckage of at least eight rail cars overturned, and considerable damage had been done to tracks and the area in general.

'I rejoined the flight and proceeded on a course from Soissons to attack aircraft on the primary target at Margny airfield. On this course the flight encountered five locomotives and one troop train running north-west from Soissons and destroyed all five locomotives and seriously damaged the troop train by strafing. On sighting a small motor convoy, the flight attacked and on withdrawing, left a truck and two half-tracks burning. Each vehicle attacked seemed to burst into flames at the first burst of machine gun fire. I assumed this to be from the two-wheel gasoline trailers attached to each vehicle concerned. During this time I strafed four fuel drums and observed many strikes, but I could not get the damned tanks to burn.

'I proceeded on from this engagement and sighted Margny airfield from 5000 ft. I observed 10+ aircraft dispersed on the north-western side of the field. I positioned the flight to attack from up-sun and made a run on six Me 109s, painted black, lined up on the outer edge of the perimeter track. I held my fire on one aircraft until it burst into flames and then strafed the remaining fighters as effectively as possible. I observed strikes on three other Me 109s.

'Having used up all my ammunition I climbed and observed the flight continuing the attack. I observed my wingman Lt Greenwood attack, and saw one enemy aircraft explode. I observed my number four man Lt Reinhardt and watched Me 109 number three burst into flames. The element leader Lt Keywan made four passes and damaged three Me 109s (shared with Capt Poindexter). The attack drew only meagre light flak to the amazement of all concerned.'

The 353rd FG flew three missions the following day, with one of them being particularly successful. Airfields in the Le Mans area were again struck, with nine Fw 190s, one Bf 109, one He 111 and one Ju 52/3m being destroyed. Two hangars, two locomotives and six trucks were also destroyed.

The 20th FG had been busy with its loco-busting activities before D-Day, and after the invasion, and the routine patrols, its pilots were eager to return to low-level attacks.

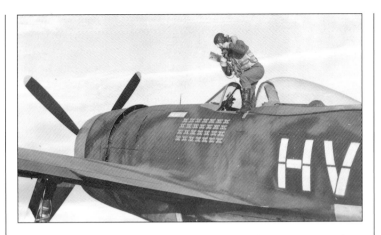

The ETO's top scoring USAAF air ace, Lt Col Francis Gabreski, vacates his P-47D 42-26418 at Boxted after leading the 61st FS on a top cover mission in support of a fighter-bomber raid on 15 July 1944. His full tally of 28 aerial victories can be seen below the cockpit of the fighter, Gabreski having claimed his last kill (a Bf 109) on 5 July. Just five days after this photograph was taken, Gabreski struck the ground with 42-26418's propeller while strafing He 111s at Bassinheim. Managing to clear the airfield, 'Gabby' successfully bellied the aircraft in nearby and was quickly captured. One of the first 'bubble canopy' Thunderbolts to arrive at Boxted, this aircraft was flown in a natural metal finish for several missions prior to being camouflaged (*via Roger Freeman*)

On 11 June the 20th sought German transport columns. One squadron flew down the west coast of the Cotentin Peninsula to Granville, where its pilots started an inland search from 1000 ft. For the next 100 minutes they had a field day. Lt Col Cy Wilson, still one of the great locomotive busters, destroyed ammunition trucks and a motorcycle and rider, with two small convoys and several military trucks also shot up.

The 355th FG went back to the airfields on 24 June. Kinnard led the first patrol, and when no aerial targets were found, the Mustang pilots sought some on the ground. Several trains were attacked before Lt Salinsky spotted a well-camouflaged fighter strip near Angers. Salinsky flamed three Bf 109s and Lt Forker two before they departed.

After the pilots returned from Angers and reported what they had found, Kinnard immediately set off to attack the strip again. On arrival, the Mustangs knocked out the flak guns and Kinnard set up a strafing pattern to enable his pilots to rake the Bf 109s from one end to the other. Twenty-five Bf 109s were destroyed and several others badly damaged.

Yet another leading ace fell to flak on 7 July. Col Glenn Duncan was leading the 353rd FG on a bomber escort mission when he spotted an He 111 on Wesendorf airfield, near Dummer Lake. Instructing the 351st FS to follow him on a strafing attack, Duncan quickly destroyed He 111 the lone but was in turn hit by light flak from the north side of the field. The oil pipe in his P-47 severed, Duncan pulled up and headed west, but he was soon forced to belly in. He radioed his group, 'I am okay, and will see you in three weeks'. But the enigmatic Duncan was to be absent for much longer, spending much of the rest of the war fighting with the Dutch resistance, and not returning to the 353rd FG until April 1945.

Eventually one of VIII Fighter Command's most successful straf-ing groups, the relatively new 339th

Ranking P-51 ace George Preddy poses for the camera after his successful action on 6 August 1944, when he shot down four enemy aircraft on one mission. His victory crosses were formed with white outlines directly onto the blue nose marking. The name which adorns 44-13321 was applied in white and black. Preddy almost certainly claimed the last of his five strafing kills in this machine on 20 July 1944 (*via Roger Freeman*)

Maj Bill Price (left) flew two combat tours with the 350th FS/353rd FG, becoming squadron CO during his second. He was regarded as a unit stalwart, having scored three aerial victories and four strafing kills while flying a P-47 and two P-51s named *"Janie"*. He is seen here with group flight surgeon Capt Joe 'Doc' Canipelli (centre) and ten-kill aerial ace Maj Wayne Blickenstaff (*via Jerry Scutts*)

FG was just getting into its stride in the weeks after D-Day. On 19 July, Maj Joe Thury led an escort mission, and on the return leg he sighted an airfield south-west of Augsburg. He led his pilots in a strafing attack, during which he and his wingman each destroyed an aircraft. The flak was intense so they held off the rest of the squadron, Thury's P-51 being hit twice in the wing root left of the cockpit.

As the unit continued home, the pilots stayed below the clouds to search for targets. Thury saw an airfield near Heilbronn and the P-51s attacked at 400 mph, destroying three aircraft on their first pass. Unopposed by flak, the pilots established a traffic pattern around the field and made four more passes, leaving 12 Ju 88s and two other aircraft burning.

Although VIII Fighter Command returned to bomber escort duty in August 1944, the fighters nevertheless remained in the ground attack business, as Capt Bill Price of the 350th FS/353rd FG recalls;

'Normally, the Germans moved supplies during the night and then hid out in the woods during the day. One morning, we took off in the darkness and arrived behind their lines at dawn. Their trucks and other vehicles were just pulling off the roads as the sun came up. We dropped

When the 352nd FG's Lt Col John C Meyer returned from leave in the United States as a newly-married man, his new P-51D also received what is believed to be its 'married name'. This photo shows *Petie 2nd* as it looked in August 1944, displaying 16 swastikas (7.5 of which were for strafing kills) and the aircraft's nickname in white, with a black outline. Meyer failed to score a single aerial victory with this machine, although he destroyed possibly as many as six aircraft on the ground with it. The fighter was passed on to Lt Sheldon Heyer in mid September 1944, and he later renamed it *Sweetie Face* (*via Michael O'Leary*)

P-47D 42-26413 *"OREGONS BRITANNIA"* was regularly flown by Col Hubert Zemke, CO of the 56th FG, from early June through to mid August 1944. In that time he destroyed 2.5 aircraft on the ground and three in the air. Following the 'Hub's' departure to the 479th FG, this aircraft was flown by five-victory ace Harold Comstock (and several other pilots), who had been CO of the 63rd FS since 19 July 1944. He almost certainly claimed his only two ground kills with it in September and November. 42-26413 was finally written off when Lt Samuel K Batson stalled in after suffering an engine failure whilst on approach to landing at Boxted following a local flight on 30 December 1944. The pilot perished in the crash (*via Jerry Scutts*)

our bombs 20 to 30 yards from the road, then proceeded to strafe the vehicles we could see. The whole area was burning from fuel, and other flammable material, being ignited by our incendiary and armour-piercing 0.50-cal bullets. Our timing had been perfect.

'We felt a genuine feeling of accomplishment, as our infantry would not have to face this stuff at a later date. In my gun camera film you can see the vehicles I hit burning briskly, and in the distance many more trucks can be seen ablaze. There were 30 or 40 of us on the mission, and we had plenty of targets to shoot up. We knew we'd done a lot of damage to the enemy's efforts to re-supply their troops.'

On 4 August the 353rd FG escorted bombers to the Hamburg area, where they encountered 70 to 100 Bf 109s attempting to intercept their charges. A big dogfight ensued, and the group accounted for 14 of the interceptors. On the return trip one element from the 353rd FG spotted 20 enemy aircraft at Plantlunne airfield and destroyed three of them.

After their return to Raydon, the pilots reported this find, and a new mission was hastily briefed. Later that afternoon, Lt Col William Bailey

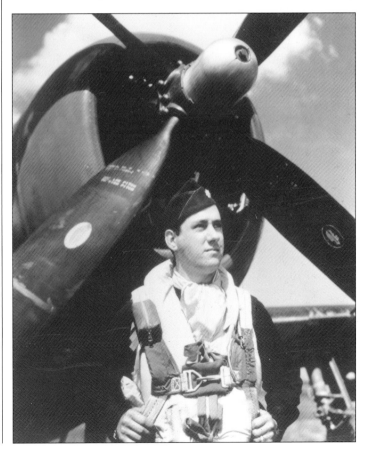

Lt Col David Schilling took over the 56th FG from Col 'Hub' Zemke in August 1944. A high scorer in aerial combat and on airfield attacks, Schilling already had 14.5 aerial victories when he opened his ground score. He achieved a 'hat trick' with three Fw 190s downed on 21 September 1944 and then scored five in one day on 23 December. His final combat tally was 22.5 aerial and 10.15 strafing kills

P-47D 42-26581 *Little Princess* was assigned to Capt Marvin Bledsoe of the 350th FS/353rd FG, and he used it to claim 5.5 strafing kills in the summer of 1944 (*via R Freeman*)

This photograph was taken by the 56th FG's Capt Harold Comstock with a K-25 camera fixed to the armour plate of P-47D 42-26413. It shows smoke rising from burning aircraft at Gelnhausen airfield on 5 September 1944. 56th FG pilots were credited with the destruction of 39 enemy aircraft during this attack (*via Roger Freeman*)

led 36 Thunderbolts in conjunction with Col Hubert 'Hub' Zemke of the 56th FG on a joint bombing and strafing mission to hit Plantlunne once again. The 56th FG dropped 250-lb bombs, destroying six He 111s, while the 353rd shot up another 20 enemy aircraft.

Capt Bill Price led 44 P-47s from the 353rd FG on a morning bombing and strafing mission on 29 August, the group finding an airfield about 30 miles north-east of Brussels, which was strafed with good results. The day's top scorer was Lt Swift Benjamin, who claimed four Bf 109s and two Me 410s on the ground, plus another three Bf 109s damaged. He reported;

'We were flying at about 100 ft when I saw what looked to be an aeroplane parked in the centre of a field at "11 o'clock" to me. Passing over it, I recognised it as a Me 109, so I pulled up and circled to the left

Capt Michael Jackson's P-47D 44-19790 *Teddy* was photographed whilst being worked on outside No 2 hangar at the 56th FG's Boxted base on 11 October 1944. Jackson had four aerial and four strafing victories to his credit when this shot was taken, and he had increased these tallies to eight and 5.5 respectively by the end of his tour. He was assigned this aircraft in mid-September 1944, and flew it until he received a P-47M in February 1945. Jackson scored the last five of his eight aerial victories with 44-19780 between 21 September 1944 and 14 January 1945. His aerial kills were marked beneath the cockpit with a traditional black cross, while his ground strafing victories (which eventually totalled 5.5) were rendered in white. Jackson completed 86 missions between June 1944 and March 1945 (*via Roger Freeman*)

and made a firing pass at it. I observed strikes on the cockpit and engine and then saw it start smoking. Pulling up and coming around in the same direction as the previous pass, I saw an Me 410 on the edge of the woods. I passed over it and came back from the other direction, giving it a short burst from about 45 degrees. It burst into flames.

'Parked on the opposite side of the field was another '410. I made a head-on pass at it and saw a heavy pattern of strikes hit the cockpit, nose and wing roots. It flamed up instantly. At "12 o'clock" to this aircraft, and across the field, I saw a group of three closely parked Me 109s. I made a semi-head on pass and got hits on all three. Leaving one ablaze, I then saw three more groups of three Me 109s, and also some single '109s, parked in the same general area at the edge of the woods while making this last pass. I made a pass at one of the groups of three and got a good burst at one, starting it smoking, and damaged a second '109 beside it to the left.

'I came around in a left hand pass at another group of three '109s and clobbered the middle one, setting it on fire. Running short of ammo, I pulled off the target and joined my group leader and started out.'

The 339th FG escorted the bombers to Nuremberg on 10 September, and on the return flight the 505th FS worked over three airfields. But the flak at Weisenberg was 'a veritable hell of 20 mm and 40 mm', which cost one P-51 and damaged several others, including Maj Joe Thury's. Forced to limp home, he turned command of the 505th over to Capt Archie Tower, who led his charges against two more airfields. All told, the squadron's score for the day was 126 destroyed and 32 damaged.

The following day the group flew an escort mission to Brimma, in Germany, and about 100 Luftwaffe fighters were encountered. The 503rd FS occupied most of them, while the 505th FS was sent back to shoot up the airfields attacked 24 hours earlier. They continued the job in fine fashion,

33

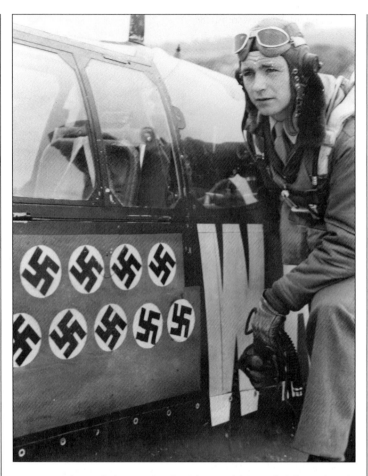

Capt Henry W Brown was the top air and ground-strafing ace of the 355th FG, claiming 14.2 aerial and 14.5 strafing kills. His most successful day's strafing came on 10 September 1944, when he destroyed no fewer than six Heinkel He 60 floatplane trainers near Frankfurt

reporting 24 aircraft destroyed and 26 damaged. Tower led the pack with five destroyed. One P-51 was downed by an Me 262 after suffering mechanical trouble and a second aircraft fell to flak south-east of Munich.

On 12 September Capt Fred Haviland Jr of the 355th FG's 357th FS, accompanied by Lts William J Cullerton and James O Juntilla, visited Schwarza aerodrome. Haviland later recalled;

'I was flying as "Custard Blue Leader" on a bomber escort mission to targets south of Berlin. A few minutes after rendezvous, the bombers were attacked by 50+ Fw 190s. During the encounter I followed an Fw 190 down to the deck, my flight still being with me. We observed the enemy aircraft land on an aerodrome with many twin-engined aircraft parked all over the field and not dispersed. The aerodrome was later identified as Schwarza. I passed by the field to a point approximately three miles north of it and then did a 180-degree turn back to line up on the aerodrome.

P-51D 44-14023, flown mainly by Capt George T Rich of the 505th FS/339th FG, displays its faded and chipped paintwork. Loaded with 75-gallon drop tanks, it is ready to be fired up and sent on its way. Rich claimed 1.5 aerial and five strafing victories in this aircraft between 10 September 1944 and 4 April 1945

'As I approached, I picked a line of parked aircraft, which were Ju 88s and either Me 110s or Do 217s. I centred my fire on two Ju 88s, but at the same time observed strikes on the other aircraft parked close by. During this first attack two flak pits opened up on me from the south-east corner of the field. I immediately turned into the gun pits and silenced both

Capt Fred Haviland of the 355th FG's 357th FS admires the kill markings being painted on the canopy frame of his P-51D (44-14402) by crew chief S/Sgt Gale Torrey. By the time he completed his combat tour in January 1945 there would be 12 of them – six aerial and six strafing victories

William John Cullerton

William Cullerton was born on 2 June 1923 in Chicago, Illinois. He entered the Army Air Force and graduated as a pilot on 7 January 1944 at Victoria, Texas.

Cullerton joined the 355th FG's 357th FS, Eighth Air Force, in June 1944. He was not long in establishing his credentials as he downed two Bf 109s on 16 August. On 2 November 1944, Cullerton and his flight again encountered German fighters and he shot down two of them. After his aerial victories he attacked an airfield, destroying six enemy fighters on the ground to begin his great strafing record. Cullerton scored his fifth aerial victory on 4 April 1945, but was shot down by flak four days later. Captured by Waffen SS soldiers, the ace was shot in the abdomen by one of his captors and left for dead. Cullerton was eventually discovered by a civilian and taken to a Catholic hospital, where he recovered.

He left the Air Force at the end of the war and became a manufacturer of fishing tackle. Cullerton's final score was five aerial and 15 strafing victories.

Lt William J Cullerton was another of the 355th FG's top aces, with five aerial and 15 strafing kills. His first big day came on 12 September 1944 when he destroyed seven enemy aircraft on the ground, but he and *MISS STEVE* did even better on 2 November 1944 with two aerial victories and six on the ground. Cullerton is seen here posing with his crew chief, S/Sgt Seidl (second from left), and armourer, Sgt Woodnail (right). The third groundcrewman remains unidentified

P-51D 44-14355 enjoyed only a short life with the 479th FG, suffering engine failure on 27 September 1944. Assigned to strafing ace Claire Duffie (8.5 ground and three aerial kills), it was unusual in having a red flight leader's band around the rear fuselage (*via Roger Freeman*)

guns. As I pulled up from this last attack, I observed the two Ju 88s, which I first lined up, on fire. I then turned 180 degrees to go back to the field, making this attack from east to west. I centred my fire on another Ju 88 and left it burning. At this point another flak pit opened up on the east side of the field and succeeded in hitting my P-51. After my aeroplane was hit, I proceeded to get it under control and headed home, making no more passes.

'My number two man, Lt Juntilla, made his attacks on the aerodrome, stringing a bit out and behind. When I was forced to discontinue my attacks, Lt Juntilla continued, making three more passes after I pulled up. On these passes he claimed two aeroplanes destroyed, which he believed to be Ju 88s, and two more unidentified twin-engined aircraft destroyed. The windshield of Lt Juntilla's aeroplane was covered with oil and his vision ahead was very poor. He did, however, observe four fires from the aircraft he claimed destroyed.

'Lt Cullerton was separated from his flight when the bombers were being attacked, so he joined up with my section. Lt Cullerton and I co-ordinated our attacks on the aerodrome. He made his passes from east to west and west to east, and Lt Juntilla and I attacked from north to south and south to north. Lt Cullerton made six passes in all on the aerodrome.'

The score for the three pilots was as follows – Cullerton, seven destroyed, Juntilla, four destroyed and Haviland, three destroyed.

Several days later the ultimately doomed Operation *Market Garden* (the airborne attack on Arnhem, in Holland) was launched, and the offensive was well supported by VIII Fighter Command. The 353rd FG was particularly busy, and on 17 September its pilots destroyed 31 flak positions and damaged another 18, with a further 33 destroyed and four damaged the following day. Claims for both days also included two locomotives, 80 railway wagons and 30 motor vehicles.

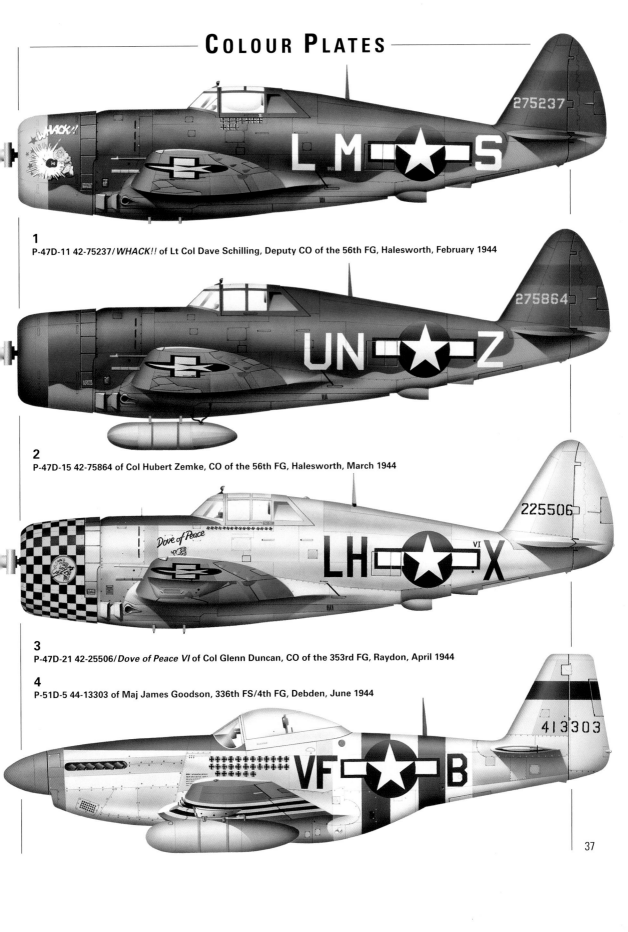

COLOUR PLATES

1
P-47D-11 42-75237/*WHACK!!* of Lt Col Dave Schilling, Deputy CO of the 56th FG, Halesworth, February 1944

2
P-47D-15 42-75864 of Col Hubert Zemke, CO of the 56th FG, Halesworth, March 1944

3
P-47D-21 42-25506/*Dove of Peace VI* of Col Glenn Duncan, CO of the 353rd FG, Raydon, April 1944

4
P-51D-5 44-13303 of Maj James Goodson, 336th FS/4th FG, Debden, June 1944

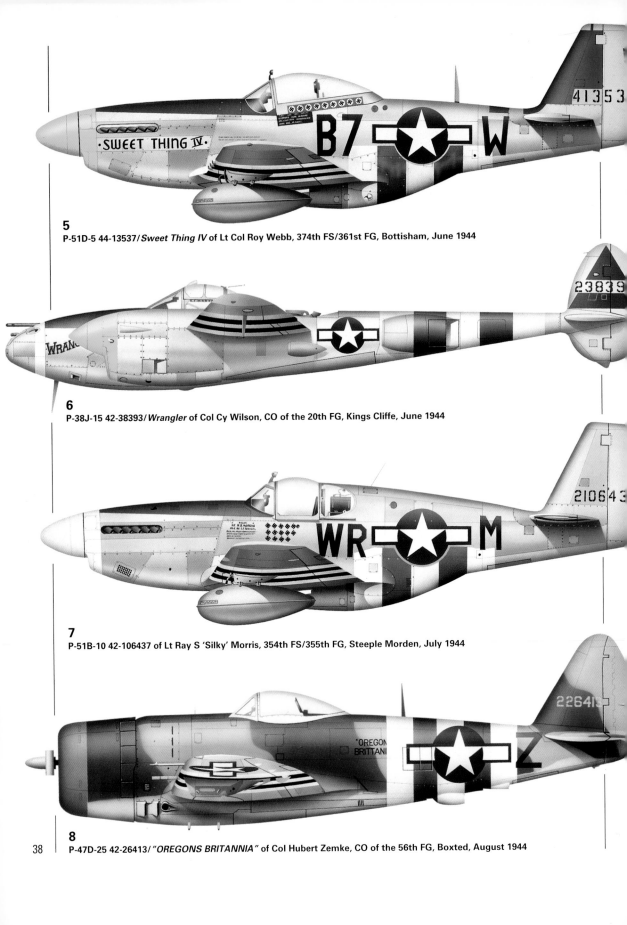

5
P-51D-5 44-13537/*Sweet Thing IV* of Lt Col Roy Webb, 374th FS/361st FG, Bottisham, June 1944

6
P-38J-15 42-38393/*Wrangler* of Col Cy Wilson, CO of the 20th FG, Kings Cliffe, June 1944

7
P-51B-10 42-106437 of Lt Ray S 'Silky' Morris, 354th FS/355th FG, Steeple Morden, July 1944

8
P-47D-25 42-26413/*"OREGONS BRITANNIA"* of Col Hubert Zemke, CO of the 56th FG, Boxted, August 1944

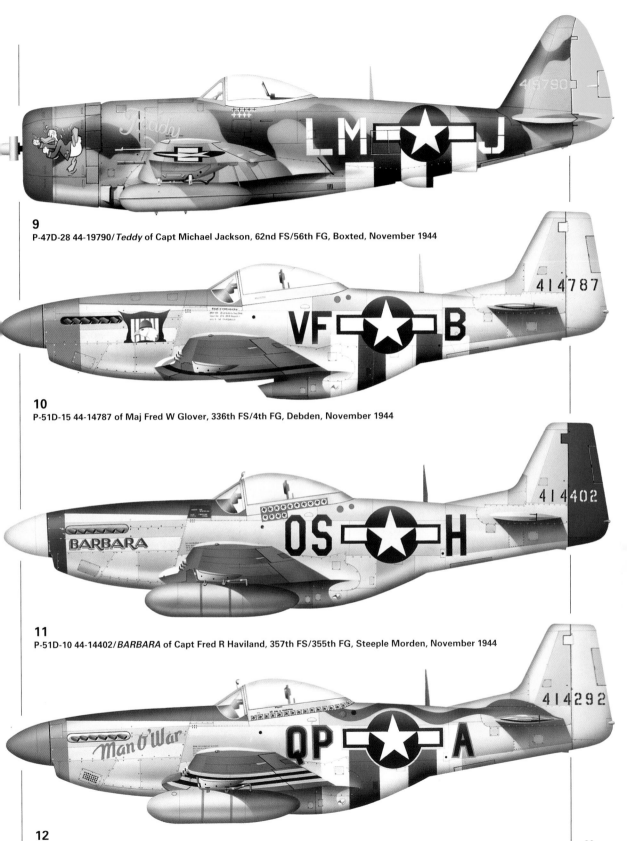

9
P-47D-28 44-19790/*Teddy* of Capt Michael Jackson, 62nd FS/56th FG, Boxted, November 1944

10
P-51D-15 44-14787 of Maj Fred W Glover, 336th FS/4th FG, Debden, November 1944

11
P-51D-10 44-14402/*BARBARA* of Capt Fred R Haviland, 357th FS/355th FG, Steeple Morden, November 1944

12
P-51D-10 44-14292/*Man O'War* of Col Claiborne Kinnard, CO of the 4th FG, Debden, November 1944

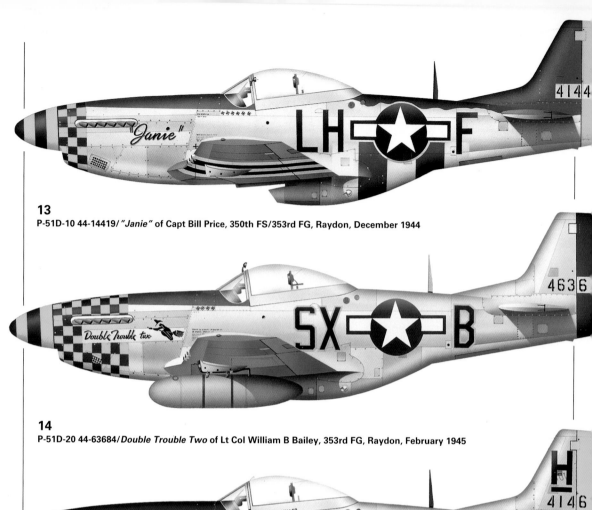

13
P-51D-10 44-14419/ *"Janie"* of Capt Bill Price, 350th FS/353rd FG, Raydon, December 1944

14
P-51D-20 44-63684/*Double Trouble Two* of Lt Col William B Bailey, 353rd FG, Raydon, February 1945

15
P-51D-10 44-14696/*HELL-ER-BUST* of Capt Edwin L Heller, 486th FS/352nd FG, Bodney, April 1945

16
P-51D-15 44-15326/*Sizzlin' Liz* of Maj Gerald Montgomery, 334th FS/4th FG, Debden, March 1945

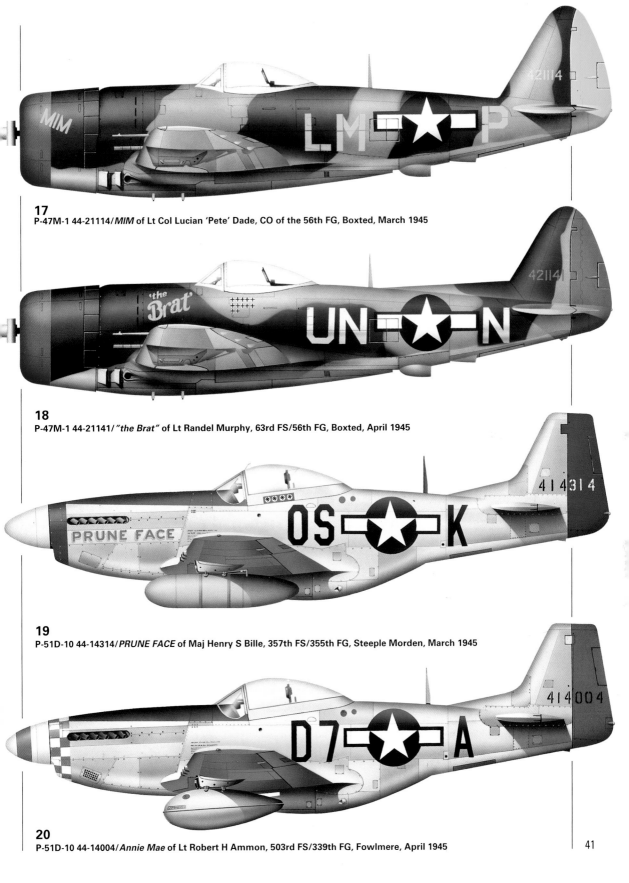

17
P-47M-1 44-21114/*MIM* of Lt Col Lucian 'Pete' Dade, CO of the 56th FG, Boxted, March 1945

18
P-47M-1 44-21141/*"the Brat"* of Lt Randel Murphy, 63rd FS/56th FG, Boxted, April 1945

19
P-51D-10 44-14314/*PRUNE FACE* of Maj Henry S Bille, 357th FS/355th FG, Steeple Morden, March 1945

20
P-51D-10 44-14004/*Annie Mae* of Lt Robert H Ammon, 503rd FS/339th FG, Fowlmere, April 1945

21
P-51D-20 44-72449/*IMOGENE* of Lt Oscar K Biggs, 505th FS/339th FG, Fowlmere, April 1945

22
P-51D-10 44-14561/*MISS VELMA* of Capt Frank Birtciel, 343rd FS/55th FG, Wormingford, April 1945

23
P-51K-5 44-11678/*BOBBY JEANNE* of Lt Col Irwin Dregne, CO of the 357th FG, Leiston, April 1945

24
P-51D-20 44-63764/*DRAGON WAGON* of Capt Jim Duffy, 354th FS/355th FG, Steeple Morden, April 1944

25
P-51D-10 44-14372/*Mary Beth* of Capt Kirke B Everson, 504th FS/339th FG, Fowlmere, April 1945

26
P-51D-20 44-63633 of by Lt Col John L Elder Jr, 357th FS/355th FG, Steeple Morden, April 1945

27
P-51D-15 44-15373 of Maj Norman Fortier, 354th FS/355th FG, Steeple Morden, April 1945

28
P-51D-15 44-14966/*Luscious Lu* of Lt Robert L Garlich, 357th FS/355th FG, Steeple Morden, April 1945

43

29
P-51D-15 44-14985/*The Millie G* of Maj Edward B Giller, 343rd FS/55th FG, Wormingford, April 1945

30
P-51D-20 44-64148 *Happy IV/Dolly* of Lt Col William C Clark, 339th FG, Fowlmere, April 1945

31
P-51D-20 44-72216/*Miss HELEN* of Lt Raymond H Littge, 487th FS/352nd FG, Bodney, April 1945

32
P-51D-10 44-14359/*Lil Lila Lee* of Capt Joseph E Mellen, 354th FS/355th FG, Steeple Morden, April 1945

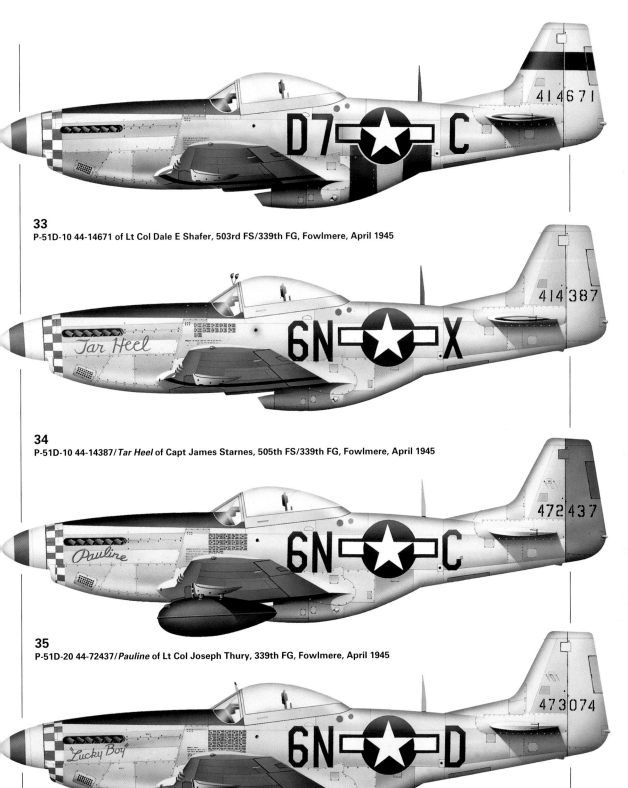

33
P-51D-10 44-14671 of Lt Col Dale E Shafer, 503rd FS/339th FG, Fowlmere, April 1945

34
P-51D-10 44-14387/ *Tar Heel* of Capt James Starnes, 505th FS/339th FG, Fowlmere, April 1945

35
P-51D-20 44-72437/ *Pauline* of Lt Col Joseph Thury, 339th FG, Fowlmere, April 1945

36
P-51D-25 44-73074/ *"Lucky Boy"* of Maj Archie A Tower, 505th FS/339th FG, Fowlmere, April 1945

45

A HARD AUTUMN

After the break-out from Normandy, the Allied ground forces began to fan out and advance into France and the Low Countries. By the autumn of 1944 they were pursuing the Germans back to their homeland, but the advance had been so rapid that the advancing armies were beginning to out-run their lines of supply, and by October the advance was beginning to slow down.

By this time most VIII Fighter Command groups had reverted back to flying their traditional bomber escort missions, leaving the tactical Ninth Air Force to fly the ground attack sorties. However, on 5 October the 20th FG was briefed for an unusual mission. It was to fly to a point north of Rostock and then continue with the bombers to Politz. On the return leg the fighter pilots were to make a low-level investigation of seaplane bases along the Baltic Sea.

The P-51 pilots found anchorages in five locations along a 150-mile stretch of coast between Stettin and Lübeck. The group had never been presented with more attractive targets, and there was negligible opposition. The pilots attacked aggressively, destroying 40 aircraft and damaging another 14 – the leading scorer was Lt Frederick Alexander with three 'He 111s' (probably He 115s), a He 115 and a Do 18 destroyed.

The 355th FG's Lt William Cullerton, the hero of 12 September, nearly repeated his feat on 2 November when Maj John L Elder Jr led the group on an escort mission to Merseburg. As the fighters moved in to cover the bombers for the return journey, four Me 262s appeared. When the Mustangs turned towards them, the jets went into a dive and lost the P-51s at about 8000 ft. Elder led the group back up to 10,000 ft, where, with good visibility, the pilots could resume the search for enemy aircraft. Finally, one was spotted low down following a railway line. The 355th went in pursuit and were led to an airfield where other enemy fighters were circling to land. The Mustang pilots pounced and shot down five before making strafing attacks.

There were about 50 single-engined aircraft scattered all over the field, some parked wingtip-to-wingtip. In the south-west corner, 15 were parked together in two rows, with camouflage nets thrown over them. They were apparently fully fuelled, as every one of them was burning by the time the group had finished. Dispersed on the north-east side were another eight aircraft, of which six were set on fire.

The attacking pilots noted that some aircraft failed to explode immediately they were hit, although they were later seen to be burning and did subsequently explode. The aircraft were parked so close together that fire spread to the others, although these were not claimed by the attackers. The 355th pilots were also surprised at the Germans' failure to disperse the aircraft, and they reported that they were even packed close together in the parking area off the field. As a result, the 357th FS alone claimed 25 single-engined aircraft (all believed to be Bf 109s and Fw 190s) destroyed on the ground. Cullerton's contribution was two aerial and six strafing

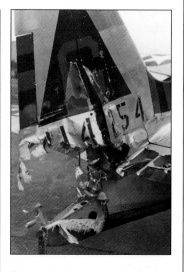

The battle damaged tail of Lt Donald Bloodgood's P-51D 44-14254. The 385th FS/364th FG pilot struggled back to base with his 'tail feathers' in shreds after his Mustang suffered a direct hit from a large calibre exploding flak shell during a strafing attack on an unnamed airfield in Germany on 24 October 1944. Bloodgood finished the war with one aerial and two strafing kills (*via Roger Freeman*)

Capt William J Sykes joined the 376th FS/361st FG in June 1944 and became an aerial ace on Christmas Eve. He was shot down just minutes after claiming his fifth kill, baling out wounded north-east of Trier. Captured, he was wounded again in an air raid on 2 February 1945. Sykes had also claimed five strafing kills prior to his capture

Henry Brown's 355th FG P-51D, with unit-applied dark green camouflage on the uppersurfaces of the wings, tailplane and fuselage decking – the paint was also taken up the leading edge of the fin. The black C on the rudder identifies the flight to which Brown was assigned. Having claimed seven strafing kills in this machine (including six He 60s at Frankfurt on 10 September 1944), Brown was shot down by flak whilst attacking Nordlingen airfield in 44-13305 on 3 October 1944. He had destroyed a Bf 110 just minutes earlier (*via Roger Freeman*)

Strafing ace William Cullerton's 44-13677 *MISS STEVE* displays 18 of his credited 20 air and ground kills. Seen here after suffering a crash-landing, the aircraft did not sustain serious damage and was repaired. Cullerton was shot down in another P-51D (44-64011) on 8 April 1945 (*via Roger Freeman*)

victories, while Elder claimed one in the air and five on the ground.

In the autumn of 1944 a new threat began to materialise – the Messerschmitt Me 262 jet fighter. With a top speed of 536 mph, the escort fighters could not hope to catch it, so their best chance would be to surprise a jet while it was taking off or landing.

It was decided that VIII Fighter Command would make sweeps against the jets, and one such mission was scheduled for 18 November when Lt Col Kinnard, who had just become CO of the 4th FG, led a mission to the jets' base at Leipheim. The group climbed to 12,000 ft, where it orbited to wait for the 355th FG, which was to fly top cover. When the force reached its target, the 335th and 336th FSs attacked flak installations.

The mission proved to be highly successful. With so many Me 262s on the ground, some of the attacking pilots were able to make as many as four passes each – they destroyed 12 of the jets, plus a Bf 109. When the 4th had completed its attacks, it was the turn of the 355th, whose pilots claimed another 14 Me 262s. Not content with that, the 355th also claimed eight locomotives, nine tank wagons and 30 troop trucks!

By December the Americans had virtually halted their advance. Seizing this opportunity, Hitler launched his last major offensive in the west – the Battle of the Bulge – in an effort to drive a wedge between the Allied ground forces and push them back to the sea. Bad weather and low cloud denied the Allied fighters the opportunity to support the ground troops, and for a while the situation looked serious. But by early 1945 the 'bulge' was closed and American forces were back on the offensive.

The Luftwaffe effectively sealed its fate on New Year's Day morning when it launched Operation *Bodenplatte*. A massed attack against airfields

Maj Fred W Glover was yet another successful 4th FG strafing ace who had previously trained with the RAF prior to transferring to the USAAF in February 1944. Glover was shot down by flak (in P-51B 42-106856) north of Valence, in France, on 30 April 1944, although he not only survived this but was back in England by 28 May. He was credited with 10.333 aerial and 14.5 strafing kills, five of the latter being scored in February 1945. Glover was subsequently killed in a post-war flying accident on 7 July 1956

in Belgium and Holland, the Germans put up virtually every fighter that could fly in an attempt to catch Allied units off-guard on the ground. Despite the Luftwaffe destroying some 150+ Allied aircraft, it in turn lost about 300 men and machines, mostly to anti-aircraft fire. Amongst those not to return were two *geschwader*, six *gruppe* and ten *staffel* commanders.

The Luftwaffe was also now running critically short of fuel. For the Allies this meant that German aircraft were more likely to be attacked on the ground than in the air. As a result, some of the biggest and most destructive 'down to earth' operations of the war would now be flown . One such mission took place on 16 January 1945 when the 4th FG, led by Maj Fred Glover, attacked Neuhausen. Glover reported;

'We were escorting the front box of B-17s from the 3rd Division on a mission to Ruhland. "Becky" squadron was free-lance, with the other two squadrons giving close support. I led the bombers by about 50 miles to Hanover, Brunswick and Magdeburg. Having failed to engage any enemy aircraft by this time, I went to the lake district south of Berlin. From there, I flew south-east to Cottbus. At this point, my green section, led by Lt Van Chandler, saw a bogie on the deck. I sent them down to engage. They lost him, but in climbing back up they saw another aircraft landing on Neuhausen aerodrome. I told them to attack. They attacked, and in two passes received no flak and had five aircraft burning on the deck by the time I got the rest of the squadron down.

'I told the other two squadrons to stay with the "big friends", and that we would be unable to join after strafing. We made seven or eight passes apiece with the exception of myself. After three passes on enemy aircraft, I made four others to take pictures with my K-25 camera. On the re-form, I counted at least 25 fires, but could not count further due to heavy smoke from the burning aeroplanes. This aerodrome appeared to be an assembly point. In the surrounding woods were a lot of silver Fw 190s, which appeared long-nosed. There were no large hangars, but blister-like Nissens on the field and along the road east of the 'drome.

'On the field itself, most of the aircraft were Ju 87s, which could have been used for training – however, I noticed no barracks, flying control or HQ building. Altogether, we were on the aerodrome about 20 minutes, but had to leave due to shortage of gas and no ammo. We did not strafe trains because of orders received prior to the mission.'

Chandler claimed four destroyed and Glover three.

The 20th FG, led by Lt Col Russell Gustke, escorted bombers attacking oil targets on 8 February. Gustke's intention was to find a target for his pilots to strafe, but cloud cover prevented this. The 77th FS, led by Maj Merle J Gilbertson, had better luck, and in a 20-minute attack on Eperstedt aerodrome, the squadron destroyed 39 aircraft, Lt 'Lefty' Einhaus and Capt Charles Cole claiming six Fw 190s apiece. Gilbertson lost most of his cockpit canopy during the attack, suffering facial lacerations, but he was able to bring his aircraft home. He left three Fw 190s burning.

The Eighth Air Force attacked marshalling yards and an armoured vehicle factory on 20 February, when the lack of any opposition left the fighters free to attack ground targets. The 20th FG went after road and rail traffic from Nuremberg, its 55th FS, led by Lt Col Robert Montgomery, heading east and south-east and almost immediately finding trucks carrying tanks and freight. After machine gunning these, Montgomery and his pilots destroyed two radio stations.

Lt Kenneth McNeel encountered a train comprising 75 trucks south of Nuremberg. The locomotive escaped because it was in a ravine, but McNeel and Lt William Peel set four vans on fire using their drop tanks. Lt Solomon destroyed at least another four. But the cost was heavy, as three 55th FS pilots failed to return. One of them, Lt Sidney Stitzer, attacked a tanker, which apparently contained a volatile liquid because it exploded with such

P-51D 44-14823 *Miss Miami* was assigned to Reps Jones of the 77th FS/20th FG, the kill markings on its canopy rail denoting the pilot's two aerial and five strafing victories. Four of the latter were achieved on 9 February 1945 during an attack on Eperstadt airfield (*via Roger Freeman*)

Aerial and strafing ace Capt Charles H 'Tink' Cole Jr joined the 20th FG in September 1944 and flew many low-level operations prior to being shot down on 25 February 1945

violence that trucks, wheels, tracks and other debris were blown high into the air. Flames shot up 700 to 800 ft and Stitzer was unable to avoid flying into them. He was seen to come out the other side, flying straight and level, but with one wheel down. Shortly afterwards his aircraft rolled on its back and dived into the ground.

Capt John S Ford was hit by flak while strafing an airfield near Nuremberg and was forced to make a belly landing. Lt William McGee saw him go in and attempted a rescue. He made a good landing, but just before he stopped he apparently ran into soft ground, causing his aircraft to nose over and bend a propeller blade. Ford raced out of a nearby wood, and after discarding their parachutes, the men climbed into the cockpit to escape. However, the P-51 could not pull itself out of the mud and the pilots fled into the woods.

The 77th FS, led by Maj Merle Gilbertson, attacked trains south-east of Nuremberg. A number of locomotives and trucks were destroyed before the pilots found a train laden with oil. They used the drop tank technique to douse the trucks with fuel and then attack with machine gun fire. Ten trucks were set on fire, and it is likely that the whole train of 30 wagons was destroyed.

As the 77th left, one flight encountered an unusual target near Straubing – a mixed formation of five Luftwaffe training aircraft in flight. Two Bf 108s and an Fw 44, Fi 156 and W 34 were immediately dispatched. Another four aircraft destroyed on the ground completed a successful day for the squadron.

Meanwhile, Maj Bob Meyer had led the 79th FS north-east of Nuremberg, where, on the line to Bayreuth, they attacked six trains and individual locomotives travelling south-west. Machine gunning and use of the drop tank technique accounted for seven locomotives destroyed and 15 trucks damaged.

Lt Dale Jones spotted an even juicier target minutes later – an airfield near the small town of Weiden that was full of aircraft. In a furious 15-minute attack, 16 enemy aircraft were destroyed on the ground, Lt Frank Strick claiming three. Although slow to respond, the defences damaged some of the attacking aircraft, and one pilot was seriously wounded.

The 20th FG had another good day on 25 February. Led by Maj Merle Nichols, the group destroyed 17 locomotives, three trucks, three horse-drawn vehicles, two staff cars and 17 lorries. But it lost one of its more enthusiastic ground strafers, Capt Charles Cole Jr. He had shown his versatility on what was to be his last combat mission, as he later reported;

'It was a strafing mission in the area north of Merseburg. On the way to the area my yellow flight lost me in some clouds, so I joined up with the other squadrons of the group. Upon reaching the area, I called my red section leader and told him to keep his section up high for top cover, and I proceeded to drop down to the deck. Very shortly I spotted two trains in a marshalling yard. I called my flight to attack. I destroyed the locomotives

P-51D 44-72160 *"Little Lady"* of the 77th FS/20th FG is pre-flighted by its crew chief. This is almost certainly the aircraft in which 'Tink' Cole achieved his five aerial and six strafing kills. These tallies included six Fw 190s destroyed on the ground on 9 February 1945 and four more Focke-Wulf fighters shot down 16 days later. He was shot down in this machine soon after claiming the last of his four Fw 190s

and my flight shot up the rest of the train. During this encounter my red section leader lost sight of me.

'I proceeded with my flight to look for another target. I flew almost directly over an enemy aerodrome and observed four Fw 190s taking off and a number of other Fw 190s in take-off position. I immediately called them in to my flight and initiated an attack on the leader. I succeeded in closing in on his tail to about 150 yards and observed hits all over the cockpit. He blew up and crashed. I then saw another '190 apparently trying to belly in. I dove on him, opening fire at 400 yards. My first shots were behind him as I saw them hit the ground. I raised my sights and saw hits around the cockpit and engine and he immediately blew up.

'As I pulled up to regain altitude, a '190 broke directly into my sights. I fired a short burst and he tried breaking right. I observed no hits, but he snap-rolled and spun into the ground. I called my flight and told them to pull out for home as there were too many enemy aircraft for us to handle. As I was leaving the area, I saw another Fw 190 with its gear down, apparently going in to land. I was almost in a firing position, so I proceeded to climb up to firing range. He saw me and broke right. I closed to about 100 yards and opened fire at 20 degrees deflection. I observed strikes on his left wing and then on his cockpit. He immediately exploded and crashed. I was withdrawing from the area when my ship was hit by 20 mm flak. It destroyed my instruments and hit my coolant. I flew on for about ten minutes and then my engine quit. I bellied the ship in.'

Having force-landed near Magdeburg, Capt Cole was soon captured.

On 27 February Maj Fred Glover led the 4th FG on a mission to Halle, which proved to be very productive in terms of aircraft attacked on the ground once the bombers were on their way home. He reported;

'I went below the overcast to check the visibility and cloud base. I then called the group down and set course due south. On the way south I crossed a railroad and sent the section down to knock out two trains. I continued on south and crossed the railroad at Jena, where more trains were knocked out. I then took the autobahn south of Jena and went west. Along the autobahn we spotted 15 to 20 trucks, which were stopped. After passing Weimar I spotted five troop columns along the right side of the road. They were almost half a mile apart, and each column was made up of about 300 troops. I gave an order to strafe them. The order was carried out and the troops did not disperse too readily, firing at us with small arms. As we came down on the columns we came across a Jerry aerodrome. This was attacked and found to be lightly defended.

'There were 70 to 80 aircraft on the aerodrome and in dispersals on the north-eastern, western and southern sides. We started our attacks from west to east. This pattern was held for about three passes when it became confused. We then tried another pattern, which took in the revetments on the west side of the aerodrome. Some of the sections had split up and were attacking a landing strip south of the autobahn and also in the woods north-east of the aerodrome. All aircraft participated in this attack. "Becky" squadron was short of ammo due to previous strafing. I ordered all aircraft off the aerodrome when they started firing tracers and had them re-form. During the re-form I counted 32 fires on the aerodrome itself and six fires on the landing strip south of the autobahn. Maj Montgomery, leading "Cobwebs", made K-25 shots of all areas strafed.'

Five 353rd FG pilots wish each other good luck for the attendant press cameras at Raydon prior to heading out on a mission in 1945. They are, from left to right, Lt Roland Lanoue (one aerial and 11 strafing kills), Maj Walker Boone (two aerial and 11.79 strafing kills), Lt Louis Lee (four aerial and two strafing kills), Lt William Agnew (no victories) and group CO, Lt Col William Bailey (three aerial and three strafing kills). All bar the latter pilot were from the 350th FS. The men are standing in front of Bill Bailey's P-51D 44-63684 *Double Trouble two* (*via Jerry Scutts*)

Once these photographs were processed and studied by Intelligence, credits were awarded for 42 enemy aircraft destroyed on the ground. Leading the pack was Lt D M Malmsten with six destroyed. Several pilots were credited with three, including Glover and Maj C E Montgomery.

The 353rd FG also had a high-scoring day on the 27th. Maj Walker Boone spotted 50+ assorted aircraft on Rohrensee airfield in the Bothas area. Boone made a quick pass, received no response, and led the 350th FS in a strafing attack which destroyed 37 aircraft. Boone himself accounted for seven while Capt Herbert G Kolb got five.

Lt Robert M Cox of the 55th FG's 38th FS had a good day on 3 March when he claimed seven aircraft destroyed in the air and on the ground. He had been on a bomber escort mission to Ruhland when he was forced to abort after his engine stopped, forcing him to drop his external tanks. The engine recovered, but because he had insufficient fuel to complete the mission he headed home. Flying at 2000 ft near Kitzingen airfield, Cox spotted two Do 217s. One was circling the field at 1000 ft while the other was just taking off at 90 degrees to Cox's flight path. The Mustang pilot made a shallow right turn and closed to about 300 yards dead astern and opened fire. After a long burst strikes were observed on the fuselage, right engine and right wing. Then the right engine burst into flames and the Do 217 rolled over and dived into the ground from 500 ft.

As Cox began his attack on the second Dornier, the German pilot tried to land. In his haste he hit the ground with one wing, causing the aircraft to cartwheel down the runway, exploding and burning as it went.

The airfield was full of aircraft parked wingtip-to-wingtip. Ground fire was mostly small arms, although there was one 40 mm gun. Cox made five successive passes at the line of aircraft parked in front of the hangars.

A good example of the hazards of strafing is provided by Lt John Courtney of the 343rd FS/55th FG. On 3 February 1945, he and his flight leader attacked a train hauling rail trucks east of Berlin. Courtney, a native New Yorker, went after the locomotive but attacked from too low an altitude and hit a tree soon after strafing the engine. He pulled up with part of the tree still stuck in his wing, the right wingtip torn off and two large holes in the leading edge of the wing. Having struggled back to base, a relieved Lt Courtney recounts his narrow escape to 343rd FS instrument specialist S/Sgt George Honcharevich

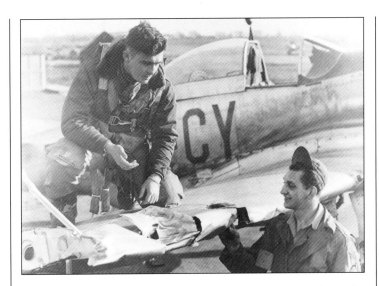

On the first, three Do 217s were set ablaze, and by the third pass the fourth aircraft had started to burn. Next time around a fifth Do 217 caught fire, together with a nearby tanker. Cox made one more pass, but only two of his guns were still functioning so he left for home.

By this late stage of the war the Luftwaffe's only real threat to the marauding Allied aircraft was the Me 262 , but there were not enough jet fighters available to mount concerted attacks on the bombers. This was partly due to VIII Fighter Command targeting the jets on their bases, or orbiting their fields to catch them taking off and landing.

There was also another new and unusual weapon for USAAF fighter pilots to contend with, although unlike the Me 262 it caused little appreciable damage. The Germans called it *Mistel*, but to the Americans it was 'pick-a-back' – a fighter, usually an Fw 190, mounted on top of a Ju 88, the

Lt Col Joe Thury was the 339th FG's top scorer, accumulating a total of 25.5 aircraft destroyed on the ground. This was his personal aircraft, P-51D 44-14656 *Pauline*, which saw a lot of hard use in April 1945, although it may not have flown during some of the final strafing missions. Photographed in late February 1945, it boasts 12 victory symbols. This style of kill marking was worn on several 339th FG Mustangs, the Nazi flags having first been printed on paper, before being glued on and varnished over

Three stalwarts of the 339th FG's 505th FS – they are, from left to right, Lt Oscar K Biggs, who destroyed 11.5 aircraft on the ground, Capt Jim Starnes, an air-to-air ace with six victories, plus another six on the ground, and Capt George T Rich, who was credited with five destroyed on the ground

Capt Jim Starnes' crew takes a rare break. Groundcrews really worked hard to keep their aircraft in good shape and capable of flying missions without having to abort them. It must be remembered that the aircraft 'belonged' to the crew chief, and that the pilot borrowed it. Starnes scored five of his six aerial victories flying an earlier P-51B named *Tar heel*. Of his 6.5 strafing kills, three were achieved in 1945, although none in this particular D-model (44-14113)

redesigned nose of which contained some 7700 lbs of high explosives. The combination was flown by the pilot in the fighter, who aimed the bomber at the chosen target. Once the compass was set, he disengaged his aircraft in flight and left the Ju 88 to fly on to the target.

One such *Mistel* combination was sighted by the 339th FG near Mockern. Lt Col Joe Thury, who had earlier been involved in chasing Me 262s after an escort mission, reported;

'About 50 Ju 88s, Do 217s and pick-a-backs were dispersed in three clumps of trees. All of the enemy aircraft were well camouflaged and parked in the wooded region, which necessitated passes from numerous angles and directions.

'Planted in the area were five or six light flak positions (0.30-cal and one 40 mm gum) which we were unable to knock out. The flak was extremely accurate and hit Lts Jones and Ziegler on their first pass. I sustained three flak hits and Lt Marts was hit once. On the first pass out of the sun, Capt Starnes destroyed one pick-a-back, Lt Ziegler a Ju 88, Lt Jones a pick-a-back and I got a Ju 88. Lt Ziegler bellied in, making a beautiful landing and was seen to get away. Lt Jones baled out from below 500 ft and hit the ground before his 'chute opened.

'Lt Marts and I were the only ones left in the dispersal area after the first pass, so I continued my attacks from out of the sun. On one pass I dropped my tanks over two Ju 88s, and in the succeeding pass one Ju 88 started to burn. I made seven distinct passes in a left-hand pattern and destroyed three Ju 88s and one Do 217, and damaged a fourth Ju 88. One of my Ju 88s exploded and burned. My other three claims burned very slowly at first, then developed into large fires which exuded black smoke, apparently from the gas in the aeroplanes.

'When we left the area Lt Marts and I counted eight fires. He didn't make any passes since he was covering Lt Jones when he baled out and continued to circle the area until I finished my attacks.'

The 353rd FG escorted the bombers to Achmer/Bramsche airfield on 21 March, and once the 'big friends' had departed the Mustangs attacked targets on the ground. Maj Walker Boone led the group, which destroyed 33 aircraft and damaged another 18 on the ground. Flying with the 350th FS, Boone shared in the destruction of six Arado Ar 234 jet bombers with his wingman, Flt

Joseph L Thury

Joseph Thury was born on 20 March 20 1919 in St Paul, Minnesota. He began aviation cadet training in June 1941 and graduated on 6 February 1942. Thury flew with a number of fighter units in Mississippi, Louisiana and Florida, before joining the 339th FG as operations officer for the 505th FS in August 1943.

Thury assumed command of the squadron in England after Maj Don Larson was killed in August 1944. He flew two combat tours with the unit and ended the war as one of the high scorers of the Eighth Air Force. He accounted for 11 enemy aircraft on the ground in April 1945.

Thury left the service at the end of the war and spent most of his civilian life practising law in Florida. His total score was 2.5 aerial and 21.5 strafing kills.

Lt Col Joe Thury, CO of the 339th FG's 505th FS, had a difficult time getting his release from instructing Stateside, but when he arrived in the combat zone he really made up for it with a total score of 2.5 kills in the air and 25.5 on the ground. This tally was achieved during the course of two frontline tours

Off Richard Gustke. Lt Roland Lanoue claimed two of the Ar 234s plus a He 111. Capt Gordon Compton led the 351st FS, which scored seven times, but lost three pilots to heavy flak.

The 352nd FS was tasked with suppressing the flak on this mission, although its pilots still managed to destroy some enemy aircraft. The squadron's top scorer, Lt Alvin Michel, accounted for four before he fell victim to flak and was forced to crash land, becoming a PoW.

Another group in the limelight during this period of continuous attacks against the Luftwaffe on the ground was the 55th FG, led by Lt Col Elwyn Righetti. The group was up in force on 21 March, and once the pilots had completed their escort duty, they turned their attention to Hopsten airfield. Righetti related;

'We were carrying 500-lb fragmentation bombs, and these were placed in the immediate proximity of the numerous gun emplacements bordering the east side of the field. After dropping my "frag", I hit the deck on the south side of the field and did two complete turns around the perimeter track. Flak was intense, and I received a 37 mm hit in the tail section. I was able, however, to locate most of the gun positions and two or three enemy aircraft parked near a large burning hangar. I called in the guns' positions and "Tudor" squadron "frag" bombed them, inflicting a momentary lull in the flak activity.

'I pulled up and out while this bombing was in progress, and determined that my aircraft was in a satisfactory condition for an attack upon the '190s, which I had previously spotted. I then approached from north-east to south-west and fired a two-second burst from 400 to 300 yards at deck level through a small shed, behind which a grounded fighter was sitting. I observed good strikes and a small explosion, and left the '190 burning brightly.

'I broke into the smoke of a burning hangar, then turned right and returned out of the sun for a fast diving pass at the only remaining undamaged aircraft that I could locate. I opened fire from 800 yards and fired to 600 yards, observing many strikes about the cowl, cockpit and wing roots. This '190 burst into flames and continued burning brightly throughout the next 10-15 minutes of circling in search of more targets. Flak continued to be intense, and since the aerodrome could not be further considered in the big dividend class, I called my boys together and we set course for home.'

Already an aerial ace with 7.5 kills, Righetti's two Fw 190s destroyed during this mission made him a strafing ace as well.

Elwyn Guido Righetti

Elwyn Righetti was born on 17 February 1919 in San Luis Obispo, California. He entered the Army Air Corps in November 1939 and graduated from pilot training at Kelly Field, Texas, on 25 July 1940. Although Righetti repeatedly requested a transfer to combat, he was not released from Training Command until he had reached the rank of lieutenant colonel in October 1944. He was then assigned to the Eighth Air Force's 55th FG to take command of the group's 338th FS.

Righetti shared a victory over a Bf 109 on 2 November 1944, and on 24 December downed three Fw 190s. He became an aerial ace on 3 February 1945 when he shot down a *Mistel*, which combined an explosives-laden Ju 88 and an Fw 190.

Righetti was an enthusiastic ground strafer, and by the beginning of April 1945 he had destroyed six aircraft on the ground. During the course of that month his attacks on aircraft on the ground were to become the stuff of legend. He destroyed six on the 9th and another six on the 16th. The next day, on his final mission, Righetti destroyed nine enemy aircraft before he had to belly land when his coolant system was damaged by flak. Afterwards, he radioed that he was alright and would see his fellow pilots in a few days. This was not to be. He was never seen again, and it has been speculated that he fell victim to attack by German civilians. Righetti's final tally was 7.5 aerial and 27 strafing victories.

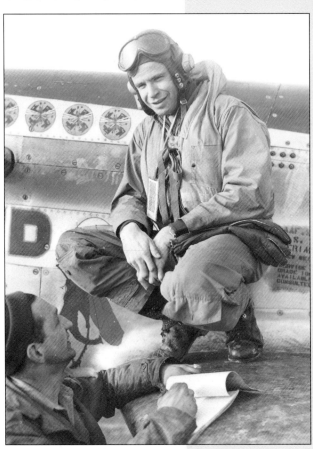

A rare photo of Lt Col Elwyn Righetti, the 'king of the strafers' and CO of the 55th FG in the final months of the war. His score of 27 destroyed on the ground was unsurpassed, and his reputation was further enhanced by 7.5 aerial victories. But he did not survive to enjoy his fame, failing to return from an airfield strafing mission on 17 April 1945. Note the elaborate and artistically-rendered swastikas to Righetti's left (*via Copeland*)

TOTAL DEVASTATION

April 1945 brought the Luftwaffe's final demise. Early in the month it committed its jet fighters in attacks 50 at a time, and there were other desperate measures like the isolated ramming of Allied bombers by a specially formed unit. But these attacks achieved little success, and VIII Fighter Command continued to flaunt its supremacy in the skies over the Third Reich as its pilots hunted down the Luftwaffe's remaining aircraft in the air and on the ground.

Despite field orders which now restricted strafing, many groups continued to take the opportunity to run up their ground scores and create new aces. These strafing attacks were among the largest and most spectacular in what is considered to be the 'down to earth' phase of VIII Fighter Command's wartime history.

One of the outstanding 353rd FG pilots was Capt Gordon Compton. Already an aerial ace, Compton would become the unit's highest scoring

The 353rd FG's Capt Gordon B Compton was the group's ranking strafing ace with 15 kills – he also achieved 5.5 aerial victories as well. Compton enjoyed great success in April 1945, destroying four aircraft on both the 5th and 16th. Additionally, he was one of the few pilots to shoot down two of the vaunted Me 262s, one on 22 February 1945 and the second on 10 April

Gordon Bryan Compton

Gordon Compton was born on 7 October 1921 in New Orleans, Louisiana. He entered the Army Air Corps in January 1942 and graduated as a pilot on 9 October 1942 at Lake Charles, Louisiana.

He joined the newly-formed 351st FS of the 353rd FG, initially flying P-40s and then P-47 Thunderbolts prior to the group moving to England in June 1943. Compton scored his first aerial victory when he shot down a Ju 88 on 22 February 1944. He was promoted to captain in April, scoring one more aerial victory and sharing another before completing his first combat tour in August.

Compton returned in November 1944 and began scoring further aerial victories, including no less than two Me 262s (on 22 February and 19 April 1945), as well as several strafing kills. He scored four ground kills on both 5 and 16 April 1945.

Compton left the service at war's end, but returned the following year. He served in a number of staff positions and was promoted to colonel in October 1965, retiring from the air force in 1968. He is now living in Wichita, Kansas. Compton's final score was 5.5 aerial and 15 strafing victories.

Maj Edward B Giller of the 55th FG poses alongside his colourful Mustang (P-51D 44-14985), which would eventually be named *The Millie G* (see profile 29). Giller was CO of the 343rd FS, and a leading locomotive buster. He also shot down three enemy aircraft and destroyed six on the ground

strafing ace during the last weeks of the war. On 5 April 1945 he led the 351st FS in an attack on Weiden airfield, the Mustang pilots circling the base a couple of times and spotting at least a dozen enemy aircraft on the ground. In the absence of flak, they decided to make a single pass on the airfield. Compton recalled;

'I picked out a group of five or six enemy aircraft in the south-east corner of the field on my first pass and set two of these (Me 410s) on fire. They were parked nose to tail. Next, I lined up three more enemy aircraft and started making passes on them. One turned out to be a dummy, one an Me 110 and the other an Me 410. After about six passes the two enemy aircraft began burning. While I was working on these in the middle of the field, my wingman, Lt Pryor, worked just to the east of me and destroyed three Me 410s, bringing the total to seven destroyed, all of which were burning when we left the field.

'On this attack I used a full load of the new APIT (armour-piercing incendiary tracer) ammunition and was not impressed with it. The tracer ammunition distracts so much attention from the gun sight that good aiming is almost impossible. The gun sight would have to be very much brighter to overcome this. Also, the minimum effective range is not more than 300 yards. Above this range the bullets tumble and spiral. This prevents any concentrations of fire to be directed at any one point.'

The 55th FG took part in one of the most destructive attacks on the Luftwaffe when, on 9 April, Lt Col Righetti led his pilots on a bomber escort mission in the Munich area. The only aerial opposition was offered by four Me 262s, and Maj Edward Giller, leading 'Tudor' squadron, hunted one down and finished it off as it attempted a belly landing at Munich-Brunnthal airfield. Giller reported;

'Having dispensed with the "blow job", and discovering that the flak was very heavy, white and red flights of our squadron flew to a 3000-ft altitude south of Munich, waiting for the bombers to knock out some of the flak on the airfield. While down there I observed a tug towing an He 111 south along the autobahn. He was heading for the woods, which were on both sides of the road. I then noticed 75 to 100 of all types of aircraft dispersed in the woods on the shoulders of the autobahn. After receiving permission to shoot up a few, I called my red flight, led by Capt Welch, to set up a pattern from west to east and then I started down.

'The first aircraft encountered was at the southern end of the woods. I got some good strikes but could start no fire. Later, I saw another aircraft, made a pass at it and set it on fire. I made a total of four passes from west to east, hitting a different target each time, all of which were parked on the west side of the road. My second pass was made on an Me 262 – I observed a good concentration of hits on the aircraft and it burst into flames. The next pass was against an Me 410 – there were strikes all over this aircraft and it too began to burn. On the last pass I hit an Me 410 and saw many strikes all over the aircraft and a large plume of heavy black smoke rising from it, but it would not burn.

'As I pulled up from my last pass, I saw the He 111 with the tug still attached, which had first drawn my attention to the concentration of aircraft. It was sitting on the north side of the woods. I put in a short burst and received in return a nice explosion and fire on the right wing root and engine nacelle. Since I was now out of ammunition, I called my flight together and we started out.'

Giller claimed an Me 262, a Bf 110 and an He 111 destroyed and an Me 410 damaged.

Capt Robert E Welch, who was leading Giller's red flight, gave the following report of his experiences on this mission;

'I took my flight further up the line and went after them from east to west. I picked out an Me 262 for my first pass and put a burst into the front – the aircraft burst into flames at once. On my second pass I chose an Me 410 to the right of the burning Me 262. I got a good concentration of hits on the wing roots and engines and this aircraft also caught fire. Pulling up from this pass, I hit a tree, damaging my right wing and putting my pitot tube out of commission. I circled before making another pass so as to allow my wingman, Lt Adams, to check over my old Mustang. It seemed okay, so I picked on another Me 262 further up the road. I saw many strikes but no fire – only damaged this boy. "Tudor" leader called that he was going home, but since I was positioned for another pass, I fired at another Me 410. This aircraft also burst into flames from hits on the left engine and wing root.'

Welch claimed one Me 262 and two Me 410s destroyed, and a second Me 262 damaged.

Capt Frank E Birtciel, who was leading yellow section in Giller's 'Tudor' squadron, arrived on the scene in time to participate in the action. His total for the day was two Ju 88s, two He 111s and one Bf 109 destroyed, and a third Ju 88 damaged. While this was going on, the group leader was busy, as Righetti reported;

'My first pass was from north to south down the autobahn. An Me 262 was destroyed on this attack, while several hits damaged an unidentified twin-engined aircraft. Pulling around in a 270-degree banking turn to the right. I made another pass, this time from west to east, destroying two unidentified twin-engined aircraft. As I broke off the attack I observed three fires from these four enemy aircraft.

'Making a 360-degree turn to port, I attacked two Me 262s from west to east in a head-on pass, destroying both. One immediately exploded,

Stained and chipped P-51D 44-14561 *MISS VELMA* was the mount of veteran ETO pilot Capt Frank Birtciel of the 55th FG, who scored five strafing kills with it on 9 April 1945

and as I closed in on the second it caught fire. I then made four to five passes on enemy aircraft dispersed along the northern perimeter of the airfield proper. Although I scored hits on several, since it was impossible for me to determine the extent of damage I make no claim.

'On my final pass I attacked two enemy aircraft – a long-nosed Fw 190 and an unidentified twin-engined aircraft parked at the north-west end of the field – in a head-on pass from west to east. The '190 caught fire, and I therefore claim it as destroyed, while the unidentified twin-engined type suffered considerable damage.'

Righetti's claims for the day were three Me 262s, one Fw 190 and two unidentified twin-engined aircraft destroyed and one damaged.

Welch had not finished his day's work. After setting course for home, he and Lt Donald E Adams passed north of Fürstenfeldbruck airfield. The bombers had just attacked, making the base ripe for a strafing attack. The two Mustangs flew one orbit before making a pass over the airfield. Flying north-west to south-east, they saw about 14 aircraft parked east of the refuelling point on the north side of the field. Adams described what happened next;

'On our first pass over the field, Capt Welch set fire to an Me 109 as the result of many strikes centred about the engine and wing roots. On the second pass Capt Welch fired a short burst and an He 177 exploded – he flew through the explosion and fired at an Me 109 sitting next to the bomber. It was left burning also.'

Welch in turn confirmed Adams' claim for one Bf 109 destroyed and one damaged during their double act. The 55th FG's total bag for the day was 49 enemy aircraft destroyed and 22 damaged.

The eager young fighter pilots continued to ignore orders to cease strafing attacks, and on 10 April there were over 300 claims for enemy aircraft destroyed on the ground, mainly from the 56th, 78th and 339th FGs.

That day saw Maj James Carter lead 63 Thunderbolts from the 56th FG on a sweep ahead of the bombers, and they duly encountered four Me 262s. One was shot down before the group broke into squadrons and swooped on airfields at Rechlin, Nuritz Lake, Neuruppen and east of Oranienburg. The fighters raked the outskirts of the fields with their machine guns while the bombers were still attacking. Another squadron hit Werder, where there were about 100 aircraft on the ground. After three passes 25 to 30 aircraft were reported to be burning.

The 10th saw massive destruction inflicted on the Luftwaffe by the 56th FG, with claims for the day including 33 twin-engined, nine single-engined and one multi-engined aircraft on the ground. Four flying boats were also destroyed at their moorings. Three P-47s did not return, although two pilots escaped after making emergency landings.

The 339th FG also enjoyed great success on 10 April, as Maj William Julian, who was flying with the 504th FS, reported;

'I chased several Me 262s but both evaded. The squadron was somewhat split up as we arrived at the target, a dispersal area north-west of Neuruppin where 100+ enemy aircraft were seen spread over ten acres of land. The upper squadron was already at work. We joined the traffic pattern and entered into the fun. It was all too easy, as there was only

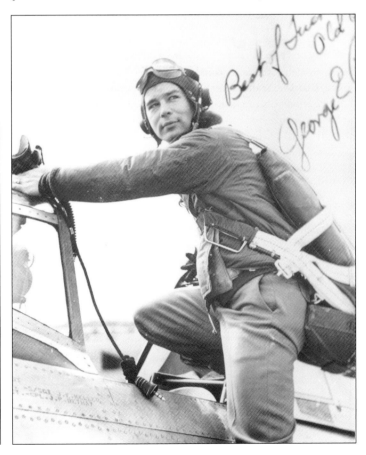

Maj George Bostwick was one of the later stars of the 56th FG's line-up. Claiming his first aerial kill on D-Day+1, he shot down three Bf 109s and damaged a fourth on 4 July 1944, and duly became an ace two days later. Bostwick also downed an Me 262 on 25 March 1945 and damaged another in April. His seven strafing victories came during the course of just two missions when he destroyed three Fw 190s at Koblenz on 8 September 1944 and two Ju 88s and two unidentified types at Werder on 10 April 1945

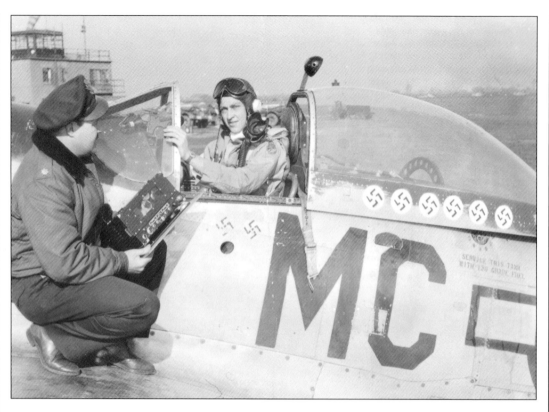

one 0.30-cal flak gun within reach of our traffic pattern, and it was completely ignored.

'Over the airfield itself was a thick concentration of 20 mm and 40 mm flak for anyone who wandered too near, but this was seldom necessary. Few of the enemy aircraft seemed to contain enough gas to explode quickly, but were evidently serviced with oil for they burned nicely once started. Eventually, the whole area became so clouded with smoke that it was exceedingly difficult to find targets.

Capt Fred Jurgens of the 79th FS/20th FG became a top strafer with eight destroyed on the ground. Note that he had two of his eight kill markings painted beneath the cockpit of his P-51D and the remaining six on the fighter's canopy rail. Note also the prominent, centrally-mounted, rear view mirror. All eight of Jurgens' victories were claimed during the 10 May 1945 attack on Werder airfield

Maj Archie Tower of the 505th FS/339th FG also claimed eight destroyed on the ground on 10 April 1945, his assorted bag of German twin-engined types being attacked at Wittstock airfield. These were his last victories of the war, boosting his tally to 18 strafing kills. The second-ranking strafing ace of the 339th FG, Tower also claimed 1.5 aerial victories

'The first pass was made at 1535 hrs and the last at 1610 hrs, with an average of ten passes being made per man. Claims were 36 destroyed and 39 damaged. Maj Julian and several others were credited with three aircraft destroyed apiece.

Lt Col Joe Thury was leading the 505th FS on the 10th, and he later related the day's events;

'We left the "big friends" just before target time. I split the squadron into two task forces, taking 11 aircraft with me and sending eight with Maj Archie Tower. We discovered a huge dispersal, which ran north from Neuruppin airfield for almost two miles. We started a traffic pattern and accomplished ten to fifteen passes, leaving only when our ammunition was low. We also made one pass on the airfield itself, which was greeted by accurate flak, but none of our 11 aeroplanes suffered battle damage. As we left, I counted 35 large fires and 20 smaller ones. The smoke curled up to 6000 ft and blanketed an extensive area. It was truly a wonderful sight!

Archie Tower flew at least two Mustangs nicknamed *"Lucky Boy"* (painted in black) during his 20 months in the ETO. This photograph, taken at the 339th FG's base 'open house' at Thorpe Abbots on 1 August 1945, shows the last of these, P-51D 44-73074, which displayed a red block with swastika markings to record Tower's 18 ground and 1.5 aerial victories. The bulk of Tower's strafing claims were made in this machine (*via Roger Freeman*)

This aerial view of 383rd FS/364th FG P-51D 44-13707 was taken over Stow Bardolph, in Norfolk, in the autumn of 1944. Assigned to John Hunter (three aerial and six strafing kills), the aircraft was shot down by a Bf 109 near Groenlo, in Holland, on 26 November 1944 whilst being flown by Lt Jack T Gaston, who was killed. By then the fighter carried the name *Lady Dorothy IV* on the left side of the nose (*via Roger Freeman*)

Raymond Smith's 44-63712 WZ-B *FLY'N TIME BOMB* carried 28 locomotive symbols denoting his ground strafing exploits shooting up rail traffic. In addition, there were eight swastika symbols on the canopy frame for the destruction of one enemy aircraft in the air and seven on the ground – officially, he was credited with five strafing kills, and these were all claimed in a P-47 (as was his solitary aerial victory). Smith flew two tours with the 84th FS/78th FG. This P-51D was lost with Lt John R Sole at the controls on 21 April 1945, the pilot being killed when he baled out too low in bad weather near Koblenz. Two other 78th FG pilots died on this mission too, 84th FS pilot Capt Dorian Ledlington being killed when he crashed as a result of the bad weather, and Lt Col Leonard P Marshall of the HQ flight perishing when his P-51 suffered mechanical failure (*via Roger Freeman*)

Lt Col Lucian Dade was the last CO of the 56th FG, and he led the group in its final big actions of World War 2, including the strafing attack on Eggebeck on 13 April 1945 – he was credited with two enemy aircraft destroyed and one damaged on the ground following this mission. Dade's final score was three aerial and six strafing victories

'I attribute our remarkable success in strafing the enemy aircraft to the fact that all upper squadron aircraft fired incendiary-type ammunition from two guns. We initiated our attack as the bombs began to fall on the airfield, which gave us perfect cover since the flak gunners had disappeared underground into shelters.'

Claims totalled 26 aircraft destroyed and 14 damaged. Top scorers were Thury and Lt Herbert Caywood with four each. Tower, meanwhile, had spotted Wittstock airfield. He reported;

'We picked out a dispersal area and set up a gunnery pattern attacking about 30 enemy aircraft parked in the woods. Enemy aircraft were also parked in front of and inside five hangars. I estimate that at least 30 aircraft were parked wing-tip to wing-tip in the area east of the hangars. We made at least 12 to 15 passes and stopped only when we had expended nearly all of our ammo. Of my section of eight aircraft, five of us were hit by light flak. There were no tracers so we weren't able to locate the guns. All my section returned home safely. It was a merry day and I wish there might be more like it.'

His unit's claims totalled 32 destroyed and 19 damaged. Top scorer was Tower with eight and Lts Robert Paul and Jerome Murphy with five apiece.

This is Eggebeck airfield under attack by the 56th FG on 13 April 1945. The group destroyed at least 95 German aircraft during this mission

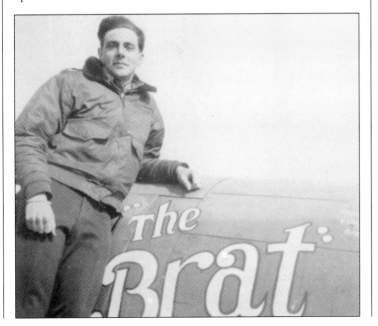

Lt Randel L Murphy of the 56th FG set the record for enemy aircraft destroyed on the ground when he was credited with ten victories following the Eggebeck mission of 13 April 1945. Murphy attributed much of the credit for his success that day to the highly volatile ammunition he used – it set everything on fire, including the grass!

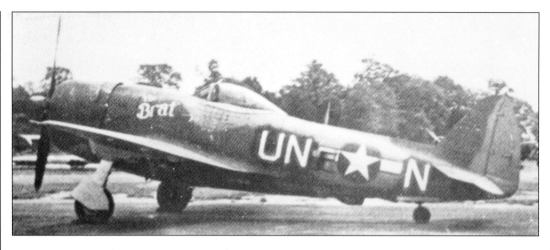

P-47M 44-21141 *"the Brat"* was the aircraft used by Lt Randel Murphy to destroy ten enemy aircraft on the ground at Eggebeck airfield on 13 April. The aircraft was finished in a two-tone blue-on-blue paint scheme relatively common amongst 56th FG Thunderbolts in the final months of the war in the ETO

As if this were not enough, Lt Col Dale Schaefer and Lt Robert Frisch, who had stayed with the 503rd FS covering the bombers, accounted for another six destroyed when they strafed the edge of the fields attacked by the other squadrons. Frisch claimed four of the total.

The 78th FG, under Lt Col John Landers' command, was also involved in the attacks. Heaviest damage was inflicted on Werder airfield, where 27 aircraft were destroyed and 22 damaged. This base was attacked by three different groups during the day, and by the afternoon American pilots were almost forced to fly on instruments to penetrate the billowing smoke rising from the airfield. The group's total claims for the day amounted to 52 destroyed and 43 damaged, with Landers top-scoring with eight. Two Mustangs did not return.

The 56th FG, under the command Lt Col Lucian Dade, had its most successful strafing mission on 13 April. The group was on a free-lance sweep of north-west Germany when it attacked Eggebeck airfield. Dade ordered his pilots to take up their respective stations, with the 62nd FS flying top cover at 15,000 ft, the 61st FS placed at 10,000 ft and the eight aircraft of the 63rd FS's blue section orbiting at 5000 ft to suppress flak that was threatening the squadron's white and red sections. Dade led the first pass down from 9000 ft, identifying three flak positions which did not seem to be manned. Opposition comprising one 20 mm gun, sited in a small village, and one 0.30-cal machine gun was easily avoided.

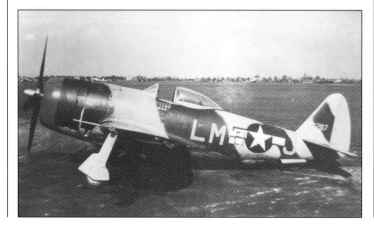

In another example of the 56th FG's experimentation with camouflage schemes in the final months of the war, Maj Michael Jackson's P-47M 44-21117 *Teddy* was painted dark green and light grey. The P-47M encountered a lot of teething troubles in the ETO, and rectifying them meant, for one thing, replacing all the ignition wiring. Jackson, who finished his tour with eight aerial and 5.5 strafing kills, failed to score a single victory in this aircraft

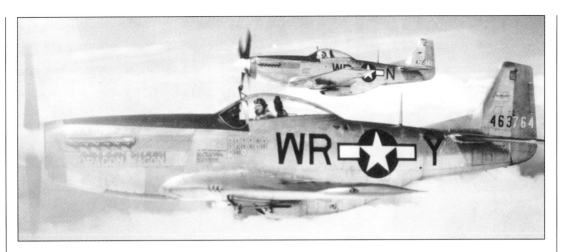

The 63rd made multiple passes until its ammunition was low. Then it was the turn of the 61st and 62nd FSs to attack. In all, the group's pilots made 339 individual passes and fired 78,075 rounds of 0.50-cal ammunition. Much of it was the new T-48 incendiary round, which had been specifically designed to ignite the Me 262's jet fuel. The 56th discovered that it worked quite well on parked aircraft too, and Lt Randel Murphy was credited with the destruction of no fewer than ten aircraft on the mission – the highest single mission strafing tally for an VIII Fighter Command pilot. He attributed much of his success on this day to the new ammunition. The 56th's total score for the day was at least 95 destroyed and 81 damaged. One Thunderbolt was lost to flak.

That same day the 355th FG destroyed 69 Luftwaffe aircraft. Maj Bert Marshall led his 354th FS away from the bomber stream to Husum airfield where he saw 50 aircraft. Seven passes were made, resulting in the destruction of 37 aircraft, with another 17 damaged. The mission's highest scorer was Lt Joseph Mellen with five.

The 355th FG's 357th and 358th FSs also strafed Schleswig, Flensburg and Lock airfields, where they destroyed a further 32 aircraft and damaged 14 others. Among the damaged aircraft were 12 brand-new He 111s which various pilots reported 'just refused to burn'.

Maj James Duffy is seen at the controls of his P-51D *DRAGON WAGON*. Two of the three Mustangs that he flew during the course of two combat tours with the 354th FS/355th FG bore this name. In the background is WR-N, with fellow 354th FS ace Maj Norman 'Bud' Fortier at the controls. Duffy claimed 5.2 aerial and nine strafing kills, while Fortier was credited with 5.833 aerial and 5.5 strafing kills

Lt Col Irwin Dregne took over the 357th FG in late 1944 and achieved a number of victories in the air and on the ground. This P-51K, which displayed the name *BOBBY JEANNE* on one side and *Ah Fung Goo* on the other, was his last aircraft, and he may have used it to score his final victories (four strafing kills) on 10 and 17 April 1945

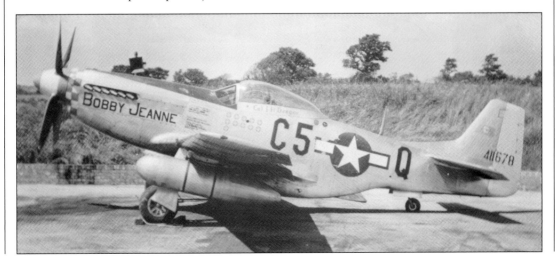

'WE REDUCED EVERY PLANE TO ASHES'

What remained of Hitler's Luftwaffe was practically wiped out over two days in April 1945. Chronically short of fuel, and with the Allied armies closing in on all sides, the Luftwaffe was now a prisoner on its own airfields. The result was total devastation, particularly on the previously untouched airfields in Czechoslovakia.

On 16 April pilots of VIII Fighter Command destroyed no less than 752 German aircraft. Most of the destruction was wrought by seven groups, and four of them each accounted for more than 100 aircraft apiece. Leading the way was the 78th FG with 135, closely followed by the 353rd FG with 131, the 339th FG with 118 and the 4th FG with 105.

In some cases the fields raided were lightly defended, but others still bristled with flak guns. The 78th FG was led that day by its CO, Lt Col John Landers, who reported;

Maj Robin Olds' rapid success as an ace in the 479th FG is well documented, but his success in strafing ground targets is less well-known. Olds scored his first five aerial kills while flying P-38s, and a further eight were achieved in Mustangs following his group's transition to the North American fighter in September 1944. He also destroyed 11 enemy aircraft on the ground, including five on 16 April 1945

Lt Col John D Landers' last Mustang, P-51D 44-72218 *Big Beautiful Doll*, is seen parked in a revetment at Duxford in late April 1945. It boasts his full kill tally of 14.5 aerial and 20 ground kills. CO of the 78th FG, Landers had previously flown P-40s and P-38s in the Pacific with the 49th FG in 1942, where he claimed six aerial kills. Sent to the ETO in April 1944, he saw combat with the 55th and 357th FGs, before becoming CO of the 78th FG in February 1945. 44-72218 was Landers' last assigned aircraft for the final months of the war in Europe, and he used it to claim 3.5 aerial and 15 strafing kills in March and April 1945. He destroyed an assortment of fighters and bombers on the ground at Werder airfield on 10 April and nine He 177 bombers at Prague/Kakowice airfield six days later

'We were providing area patrol in the Pilsen/Prague area for the 3rd Bomb Division. I flew with the 84th FS as group leader. We arrived in the area at 1430 hrs, looked over several bare fields, then checked Prague/Kakowice aerodrome, observing 80+ aircraft of all types. We dropped down to 3000 ft and flew over the field from north to south to check for flak. Two squadrons – the 84th and 83rd – continued south until out of sight, made a 180-degree turn and hit the deck. The first pass was made from south to north to give the 12 to 14 light flak guns a 90-degree deflection shot. "Jerry" had his aircraft dispersed in groups of two to five all the way around the field, with singles located in various scattered revetments.

'On my first pass I picked out four He 177s lined up in a row. Two lighted up as I fired, and after pulling up I observed all four burning. I claim only two destroyed – the other two were possibly fired by another pilot. My second pass was from east to west on two more He 177s. Both burned. The first eight P-51s across the field set 13 aircraft on fire. After four passes had been made, I counted 50+ fires on the perimeter, and there were a few more going in isolated dispersals.

'We set up an east to west pattern and, methodically, we reduced every plane to ashes. My third pass set two more on fire. From then on we picked out singles, and on my next five passes I destroyed three more. Four or five more that I damaged were later destroyed by others pilots. I got solid hits on two which were blown up by the man behind.

'When I left, there were only three aircraft still intact, and a flight went down on them to make it 100 per cent. I claim nine He 177s destroyed on the ground.'

The smoke billowing up from the burning aircraft at Kakowice was so thick that some of the 78th's pilots moved to Letany airfield two miles away, where another 50 aircraft were found and attacked. When the day's final count was made, the 83rd and 84th FSs had achieved equal scores

John Dave Landers

John Landers was born on 23 August 1920 in Wilson, Oklahoma. He gained a reputation as an accomplished football player in Texas and Arkansas, before joining the Army Air Corps. He graduated from pilot training on 12 December 1941.

Pilots were desperately needed in the Pacific, so Landers was sent to Australia to join the 49th FG's 9th FS. Once in the Pacific, he flew P-40s and P-38s and scored six kills against the Japanese. Landers was shot down in December 1942 but survived, and returned to the US shortly afterwards.

In April 1944 Landers joined the 55th FG in England, where as a captain and squadron operations officer he resumed combat flying with P-38s. When he left the 55th FG he was a squadron commander, with the rank of lieutenant colonel, and was credited with four German aircraft destroyed in the air and five on the ground.

Landers then spent a short time with the 357th FG while its commander was on leave, during which time he downed a Bf 109 and destroyed another on the ground (both on 18 November 1944).

He returned for his third combat tour as CO of the 78th FG in February 1945, downing three more Bf 109s and sharing in the destruction of an Me 262 the following month. Landers also achieved success in strafing attacks, destroying nine aircraft in the 16 April 1945 raid. He left the service at the end of the war and spent many years on overseas assignments with a construction company.

'Big John' Landers died following a surgical operation on 12 September 1989. His final score was 14.5 aerial and 20 strafing kills.

This official photograph of Maj John Landers sat in the cockpit of a 55th FG P-38J was taken at Wormingford in the summer of 1944. One of the USAAF's great fighter pilots, 'Whispering John' Landers had already 'made ace' on P-40Es in the Pacific as long ago as Boxing Day 1942 when he joined the 38th FS/55th FG in April 1944. He added a further four kills (a Bf 109G on 25 June and three Me 410s on 7 July) and a damaged (another Bf 109G) to his tally whilst flying the P-38J-15, rising to command the 38th FS in early July 1944. Landers' final 4.5 aerial and 15 strafing kills were scored with the P-51D whilst on his third combat tour (as CO of the 78th FG) in March-April 1945 (*via John Stanaway*)

with 58 destroyed apiece, while the 82nd had 19. Besides Landers, the high scorers were Lt Clyde Taylor with eight, Capt Edward Kulik with seven and Lt Col Olin Gilbert and Lt Anthony Colletti with six each. No pilots were lost on the mission.

On the afternoon of the 16th the 353rd FG struck at airfields in the Munich area, and at 1455 hrs the 351st FS commenced a 30-minute strafing attack on Kircham airfield. Between 1530 and 1600 hrs, the 350th FS strafed Pocking airfield, and at 1545 hrs the 352nd FS attacked Bad Aibling. The result was more heavy losses for the enemy, as Capt Gordon Compton of the 351st FS related;

'I located Kircham landing ground at 1455 hrs and took the first flight down on it after orbiting it once. There were 40+ enemy aircraft dispersed

Veteran P-38 pilot Capt Ernest 'Ernie' Bankey was the 364th FG's second ranking ace in the ETO, flying initially with the 385th FS before moving to the group HQ in December 1944. He increased his score from two to 9.5 aerial kills whilst serving with the HQ, and also claimed eight ground strafing victories. The bulk of his kills came in P-51D 44-15019, although his final two aerial successes were scored in the immaculate *Lucky Lady VII* (44-73045), which appears to have been recently fitted with replacement lower nose panels (*via Michael O'Leary*)

along, and in, the wooded area, and very little flak was encountered at first. The first passes were made from east to west, then from west to east and finally from south to north.

'I was the first man to make a pass at Kircham landing ground, and chose as my target a Ju 88 parked next to a wooded area in the southern part of the field. My passes at this enemy aircraft were made from east to west. It began smoking after the first pass, and after the fourth or fifth it was burning brightly. Yellow section then changed the pattern about the field so that passes would be made from west to east. My next target, another Ju 88 parked on the southern part of the field, began burning after two or three more passes. Next, I made my passes from the north at two enemy aircraft that were parked close to the wooded area south of the field. I made about six passes at these two enemy aircraft – one burned and

A two-tour, 118-mission veteran of the 353rd FG, Frank Emory served with the 351st FS from December 1942 through to April 1945. Seen here in early 1944 whilst still a young lieutenant, Emory would score two aerial and ten strafing kills, four of the latter being claimed on 16 April 1945 (*via Graham Cross*)

one exploded. The aircraft were
Ju 188s.

'Next, I discovered four or five
enemy aircraft parked along a
wooded area in the eastern part of
the field. I could not identify these
aircraft. The first of these I had no
luck with after two passes, and the
same was true for two of the others,
although one began to smoke a
little. The fourth of these exploded
on the third pass I made at it.'

Compton claimed two Ju 88s,
two Ju 188s and one unidentified
enemy aircraft destroyed. Other
high scorers were Lt Gerald J Miller
with six Fw 190s, two Bf 109s and a
Do 217, Col Ben Rimerman with
three Fw 190s and a Bf 108, Bf 109
and a Ju 87, and Capt Herbert G
Kolb with five Fw 190s, two Bf 109s
and one and three shared Fi 156s.

The 339th FG ran up its massive
score attacking airfields in the
Regensburg area, claiming 118
enemy aircraft destroyed. Capt Bob
Ammon of the 503rd FS was leading

a four-aircraft flight which attacked Prague/Kbely airfield. In the next few
minutes he would destroy nine enemy aircraft on the ground, and on his
return he explained how he did it;

'I was leading a flight on my first pass over the edge of the field to draw
flak when I shot up an He 111. As I went I spotted two flak positions,
which we shot up on our second pass, and then set up a 180-degree traffic
pattern. We really went to work on the parked enemy aircraft, and

Yet another stalwart of the 353rd
FG, Lt Col William Bailey served
with the group from October 1942
through to September 1945. In that
time he completed 186 combat
missions, flying initially as CO of
352nd FS and then transferring to
the HQ flight in July 1944. He was
credited with three aerial and three
strafing kills (*via Graham Cross*)

Lt Robert H Ammon flew with the
339th FG's 503rd FS and completed
two combat tours with the unit,
scoring aerial victories in 1944 (one
in June and four in September). His
strafing success came on 16 April
1945 when he claimed a record
11 enemy aircraft destroyed on the
ground, of which he was credited
with nine. Unusually for an ace in
terms both of aerial kills and aircraft
destroyed on the ground, Ammon
was never awarded the
Distinguished Flying Cross

Lt Col William C Clark of the 339th FG became a strafing 'ace in a day' when he destroyed six enemy aircraft during the mission of 16 April 1945. Clark finished the war with one aerial and eight strafing victories

I counted 24 fires before the Duxford squadron (78th FG) came in and started shooting up everything in sight! They did not ask to join us, or try to join our pattern, but came in from all directions. They forced me to break off two passes and endangered my whole flight. We finally got the traffic organised and made about three more passes before I got hit. My cockpit filled with smoke, so I called off my flight and headed for home.'

Already a five-kill aerial ace, Ammon's official tally for this mission comprised four Bf 109s, three Ju 88s and a single Fw 190 and He 111 destroyed – he also claimed a second Fw 190 and He 111 destroyed, but these remained unconfirmed. One of Ammon's pilots, Lt Steve Chetneky, got six kills, as did Lt John Byers.

Lt Col William Clark led pilots of the 339th FG's 504th FS to Klatoby airfield, but there were few aircraft to attack, so he detached a small force to take care of them and proceeded with the rest to Bedejovice airfield, where several hundred aircraft of all types were found. Clark reported;

'These enemy aircraft covered the whole field. Quickly planning an attack for flak, we came in low from the south with the sun at our backs. The aircraft on this field burned quickly after a very few rounds were fired – just as I was passing over one enemy aircraft it exploded, blowing the crew chief, who was in the cockpit, over my left wing! A large piece of the Fw 190 then hit my wing on the left side. By this time the flak was very heavy, so I called the section and told them not to make any more passes as the flak was too thick. Because of the flak, only four enemy aircraft were destroyed on this field. I then found another field near Platting with a

great number of aircraft dispersed around it. Going in to check for flak, we destroyed a number of Me 109s and Fw 190s. Flak was too heavy so I quit the field, and south of the town found another dispersal area. Again there was heavy flak, so we made one pass at Straubing aerodrome and headed home.'

Clark claimed three Fw 190s, two Bf 109s and one Ju 52/3m destroyed.

A total of 48 aircraft had been accounted for on the fields attacked. the 339th FG's final squadron, the 505th FS, had split up over the target area and attacked three further airfields, destroying 39 more aircraft. Remarkably, the group suffered no losses on this day.

Prague/Kbely airfield was the target for the 4th FG on 16 April, the group being led into action led by Lt Col Sidney Woods. The force comprised 'Becky' (336th) and 'Caboose' (335th) squadrons, combat veteran Maj Pierce McKennon leading the latter unit in a port orbit of the airfield in search of flak positions. Lt Harold Frederick was leading 'Becky' Squadron's green section, and he recalled;

Lt Col William C Clark's P-51D 44-64148 *Dotty* provides the backdrop for the Easter service at Fowlmere in April 1945. Also nicknamed *HAPPY IV* (see the small black rectangle below the exhaust stubs), this aircraft was used by Clark to destroy eight aircraft on the ground – six of them on 16 April 1945 – and one in the air. Clark had become the 339th FG's final wartime CO just 48 hours prior to claiming his six strafing victories (*via Jerry Scutts*)

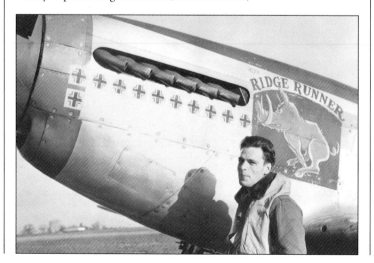

Maj Pierce McKennon was trained in the RCAF and joined the 335th FS in February 1943. He opened his aerial scoring by shooting down an Fw 190 on 30 July 1943 while flying a P-47. By the end of his first combat tour McKennon had scored 10.5 aerial kills, and been made CO of the 335th FS. There was just one more shared victory to come before the end of the war following his return to combat in early 1945, again as CO of the 335th, although he scored six ground kills in April. McKennon's final tally was 11 aerial and 9.68 strafing kills – six of the latter were claimed on 9 and 16 April 1945

A veteran of 560 combat hours in the ETO, Maj McKennon got through a number of fighters (always coded WD-A) whilst serving with the 4th FG, including two Thunderbolts and six Mustangs. This particular example was used by McKennon in the final weeks of the war, and displays his full victory tally below its port exhaust stubs

Maj Gerald Montgomery's *Sizzlin' Liz*, seen at Debden in 1945. Although Montgomery was a long-time member of the 4th FG, little is known about his exploits. He may not have run up a high score of aerial victories but he certainly got the job done on the deck

'We approached Prague on a course of 90 degrees at 10,000 ft, and after turning south on the west side of the city, we went into a shallow dive and circled it to the south. By the time we reached the east side, we were on the deck. Col Woods said he was making a starboard turn, and I was one of the first to leave the aerodrome, having expended my ammunition.

'There were about 100+ ships parked on the Prague/Kbely aerodrome, and about 60+ on the Prague/Oakevice and Prague/Letany aerodromes. There were also 15+ parked in adjacent fields. It seemed to be a receiving point for all types of aircraft. Flt Off Baugh circled the aerodrome after his last pass and counted 58 fires. Lt Douglas Pederson, who was one of the last men to leave the area, counted 60 fires. Seven pilots from "Becky Squadron" are missing in action and no claims are made for them, with the exception of Capt Carpenter and Capt Alfred.'

Of the pilots lost (all of whom fell to flak), two were killed and the others became PoWs, including Lt Col Woods. The total score for this

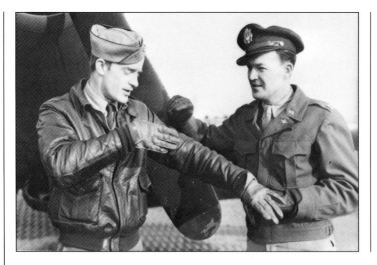

The 4th FG's Maj Louis H 'Red Dog' Norley demonstrates to Capt Ben Ezell, also of the 4th FG, just how he got that Fw 190 in the traditional fighter pilot manner. Norley was RCAF-trained, and he joined the 336th FS in July 1943. He later became CO of the 334th FS and then the 336th FS. Norley was credited with 10.333 aerial and five strafing victories, four of the latter coming on 16 April 1945

operation was 61 aircraft destroyed, and the top scorer was Lt Pederson with six Ju 52/3ms to his credit.

Maj Louis Norley took the 4th FG's 'B' group to Gablingen airfield. There, the going was much easier, and the raiders destroyed 44 aircraft for no loss. Norley reported;

'All sections pulled up in line abreast. We made the first pass from south-west to north-east. Maj McKennon called and said that he could see no flak. We pulled up to starboard and came in for the second pass. After the second pass Col Woods pulled up in a port turn and said to establish a left-hand pattern, which put us over the main flak batteries. On my third pass I observed several columns of smoke and several more beginning to burn. After the pass I heard Col Woods say his oil pressure was down to zero and he was baling out. I also heard Capt Carpenter say he was baling out too. I saw a ship going south of the aerodrome losing coolant. I followed it and identified it as Capt Alfred's ship. I lost sight of the ship for a few seconds while in a turn in which he could have baled out. After completing the turn, I observed the ship in a shallow dive streaming coolant, until it hit the deck and exploded on impact.

Maj Norley sits in the cockpit of his smartly marked *Red Dog XII* soon after the 16 April attack on Gablingen, where he destroyed four aircraft on the ground. It is possible that Norley used this aircraft (his last P-51D) to claim these kills

Maj John L 'Moon' Elder was one of the original 357th FS/355th FG pilots, being an early scorer with an Fw 190 downed on 21 February 1944. Elder became the squadron's CO in June 1944 and remained in command until the end of the war. He was credited with eight aerial and 13 strafing victories, five of the latter being gained on 2 November 1944

This is Col Claiborne Kinnard's last *Man O'War* following his return to the European theatre in February 1945 to become CO of the 355th FG. In contrast to the markings on his other aircraft, the kill symbols that adorn this P-51D have been applied along the edge of the anti-glare panel on the nose. Kinnard claimed 2.5 strafing and two aerial kills in this machine on 13 and 20 April respectively, taking his final tally to eight aerial and 17 strafing victories

'Flying back to the aerodrome, I heard Lt Ayer say he was baling out. Approaching from the south, I counted 26 columns of smoke, and in some cases two or three aircraft were in the same smoke column. This cannot be taken as a total count.'

The three squadrons of the 355th FG had also split up prior to conducting their strafing attacks, and all had been quite successful. Lt Col John 'Moon' Elder took the 357th to three fields in the Linz area, where his pilots claimed 29 destroyed and 36 damaged for the loss of two P-51s.

Capt Lawrence Dissette led the 358th to Straubing, which was stoutly defended. The attackers destroyed 18 aircraft and damaged six, but lost four pilots (two captured and two evaded) for their trouble. A fifth pilot managed to reach friendly territory before he bellied in. Meanwhile, Maj

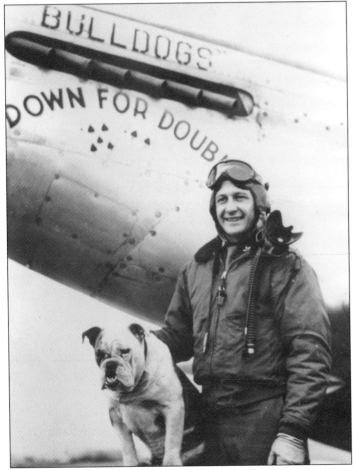

P-51D 44-14966 was the second Mustang to be named *Luscious Lu* by Lt Robert L Garlich of the 357th FS/355th FG. He destroyed 6.5 aircraft on the ground between January and April 1945, although it is unclear just how many of these kills were claimed in this particular Mustang

Lt Col Gordon M Graham joined the 355th FG in the autumn of 1944 as a major, and gained his first aerial victory, over an Fw 190, on Christmas Day. On 14 January 1945, he downed two further Fw 190s to become an aerial ace. Graham flew an elaborately decorated Mustang named *DOWN FOR DOUBLE* (P-51D 44-14276) in which he not only led many escort missions, but also airfield strafing attacks. He finished the war with seven aerial and 9.5 strafing kills

Gordy Graham met with better success at Eger and Gog, the 354th FS claiming 23 destroyed and six damaged without loss.

The 55th FG was also back in the thick of things on 16 April. It, too, split into squadrons and attacked a number of scattered airfields. Lt Col Righetti led the group down the Danube Valley from Linz to Landshut, strafing airfields along the way. One who found a hot target that day and had a narrow escape was Maj Edward Giller. His 343rd FS arrived over Brunthal landing ground, but there were not enough targets, so he allowed his flights the freedom to hunt elsewhere. Giller then separated his own flight into elements and began making passes parallel to the autobahn. On his first he fired a good burst at an He 111, which immediately burst into flames. He shifted his fire to a Bf 109 parked just beyond the Heinkel, and a solid burst set it belching black smoke as he zoomed over it. Giller then returned to the edge of the road, where he found a Ju 52/3m. He reported;

'I fired at it, pretty well covering the engines – it also burst into flames. I had to make a third pass to position myself on a target which I had observed. It turned out to be a Ju 88; I came in on it in the same pattern from south to north, and although I observed many strikes all over the aircraft, I could not get it to burn. As I pulled up from this last pass, a 20 mm flak shell came flying through the left side of my canopy and exploded, wounding me in the left shoulder. I was dazed and bleeding rather badly, so I called my flight together and we set course for home.'

Giller claimed three destroyed and one damaged. By the end of the day the 55th had destroyed 52 enemy aircraft and damaged 26 for the loss of three pilots.

Lt Col Willie O Jackson was leading 24 Mustangs from the 352nd FG when his pilots discovered about 70 enemy aircraft dispersed on Ganacker airfield. Jackson said;

'We decided to hit the aerodrome, with one section drawing flak, another busting flak and the other as top cover. I took my flight across from south-west to north-east, not firing, and 15 to 20 guns opened up. After four or five passes they were neutralised by the flak busters, and a gunnery pattern was then set up.'

For the next 30 minutes the Mustangs worked the field over from end to end, leaving 40 aircraft ablaze and another 27 damaged. The highest scorer was Capt Ed Heller with seven, while Lt C A Pattilo destroyed six and damaged another.

Edward Giller's penultimate *The Millie G* (44-63204) was written off in this accident at Kaufbuaren airfield, in Germany, on 14 September 1945. The strafing ace's 55th FG remained in Germany well into 1946 (*via Roger Freeman*)

THE FINAL RAID

The last of the big airfield strafing raids came on 17 April 1945, just 24 hours after pilots of VIII Fighter Command had achieved their greatest success of the war in terms of enemy aircraft destroyed. The day's tally was 286, following on from the stunning 752 claimed on 16 April.

Maj Wilton Johnson had led the 352nd FS of the 353rd FG on a bomber escort mission, and he later parted company with the 'heavies' and took his Mustangs down to attack Muldorf airfield. Opposed by plenty of flak, Johnson decided against hitting the base, and the squadron continued on to Ganacker, where its pilots made six or eight passes and left 19 enemy aircraft destroyed and 22 damaged. Flak accounted for two of the attackers, but one pilot was able to crash-land and the other baled out.

That same day, Capt Ray Littge led the 352nd FG to Plattling airfield, where 75 aircraft were sighted parked around the field. Littge subsequently reported;

'Red flight made several passes at flak positions first, effectively silencing them. During these attacks one of my oil tanks was hit and I lost most of my oil. One of my guns was also shot out and two electrical lines and the manifold pressure line were holed. Ignoring the damage, I made seven passes in total. My first two were at an Me 262 in the north-east corner of

Capt Raymond H Littge of the 487th FS/352nd FG liked multiple victories, both in the air and on the ground. His aerial kills came as two Bf 109s on 27 November 1944, three Fw 190s on 27 December 1944 and another two Fw 190s on 1 January 1945. He was eventually credited with an aerial score of 10.5. Littge's ground kills totalled 13, with three scored on 15 April and six the following day

Capt Kirke Everson of the 504th FS/ 339th FG shared in the destruction of an Me 262 in the air on 4 April 1945 and destroyed 13 Luftwaffe aircraft on the ground during that month. His big day came on 17 April, when he finished off seven of them at Klatovy/Anberg

the field, which blew up after the second pass. I then attacked and set fire to an Me 109 on the north side. On each of my next three passes I set fire to Me 109s in revetments on the south side of the field. And on my last pass I blew up another Me 262 in the north-east corner of the field. When we left the field there were at least 70+ fires.'

That day the 352nd destroyed 66 aircraft and damaged a further 24. Although Littge's Mustang was holed by flak, he topped the scoring with six, while Lts James White and Karl Waldron were each credited with five apiece.

The 339th FG also had a good day on the 17th, with 67 aircraft destroyed on the ground and nine damaged. As usual, the squadrons separated for the attack. Lt Col Thury reported;

'With 18 aircraft, we discovered and hit a dispersal area just south-west of Pocking with 50+ enemy aircraft in the area, dispersed among clumps of trees and excellently camouflaged. Some of the enemy aircraft exploded, but most started to burn, very slowly at first, before developing into raging fires. We counted claims only after observing positive fires. When we left there were 25 huge fires and 14 smaller ones, and smoke was curling up to 6000 ft. I'm convinced that some of our claims would not have caught fire were it not for the fact that all my ships had two guns firing incendiary ammo. There were two 20 mm and one 40 mm guns firing at us during the attack. Lt Irion knocked out one 20 mm position. The remaining gunners were not too eager after that.'

Thury destroyed five, but the 339th's top scorer that day was Lt Leon Orcutt with eight.

The 55th FG, led by Lt Col Righetti, escorted bombers from the 3rd Air Division to Dresden. The weather was bad, but towards the end of the mission the Mustangs were able to drop through the overcast, and some

81

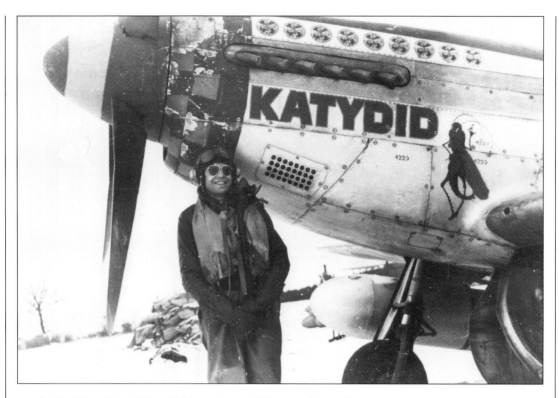

caught Fw 190s taking off from fields in the area. Nine were downed in aerial combat before the air-to-ground shooting began.

Capt Carroll Henry was flying Righetti's wing as they went through a hole in the clouds and prepared to test the flak on Riesa/Canitz airfield, which appeared full of parked aircraft. Just as Henry was about to make his first pass, Righetti told him to take care of an Fw 190 which was preparing to land. While the colonel made his attack on the airfield, Henry downed the Fw 190. He reported;

'When I had destroyed the '190, I took a quick look at the field to locate the colonel before making any passes myself. I observed fires from three Me 109s at this time. I made a pass from north to south on a large dispersal area north-east of the airfield. I got in a two-second burst at an unidentified single-engined aircraft and saw it burst into flames. I pulled up and saw Col Righetti making a strafing pass, his aeroplane streaming coolant. He now had seven fires burning.

'He called over the R/T, "This is Windsor. I'm hit bad, oil pressure dropping. I can't make it back. I have got enough ammo for one more pass". I watched him make that pass and obtain good hits on two more aircraft. I could not watch for fires as I wanted to give the colonel cover on any move he might make. After his pass he pulled up slightly and levelled off on a course of 270 degrees, flying about five miles before belly landing in an open field. After he was on the ground I received the following message over the R/T. "I broke my nose but I'm okay. I got nine today. Tell my family I'm okay. It has been swell working with you gang. Be seeing you shortly".'

The nine aircraft destroyed would take Lt Col Righetti's final score to 7.5 aerial and 27 strafing kills. But there would be no reunion, for

Lt Col Elwyn Righetti and his personal aircraft, P-51D 44-14223 *KATYDID*, pose in the snow at Wormingford in January 1945. From its general appearance, it is obvious that this aircraft had seen a lot of action during the winter of 1944-45

384th FS/364th FG ace John Lowell called all his personal aircraft *PENNY*. This was his last P-51D, which bears 17 swastika victory symbols for 7.5 aerial and nine strafing kills. The fighter's original rudder was repaired or replaced at some point, as the last three digits (263) of the tail number were missing on the left side and the first three digits (463) were absent from the right side! The strange shaped letter L (for Lowell) on the tail was seen on earlier aircraft in this squadron, suggesting use of the same stencil (*via Roger Freeman*)

Col Hubert 'Hub' Zemke, CO of the 56th FG, led his group on many strafing missions. He believed in such attacks, but not in giving credit to individual pilots for destroying aircraft on the ground. While his pilots were very disciplined, it is said that Zemke once posed as an enlisted man in order to enter a boxing match!

Righetti was never heard from again. It was assumed that he met his death at the hands of angry civilians. He was one of five 55th FG pilots who did not return that day, and only one would subsequently emerge from a PoW camp post-war.

To all intents and purposes the attacks of 17 April represented the last big airfield raids carried out by pilots of VIII Fighter Command. Further claims were made the following day, but these 12 would be the last of the war.

The command had initiated the policy of attacking the Luftwaffe on the ground early in 1944 to further its objective of winning air superiority. The focus had shifted to the enemy's ground transportation as part of the softening up operation before the Normandy landings in June. During this phase American pilots destroyed hundreds of railway locomotives and much rolling stock, together with other vehicles, both armoured and soft-skinned. The attack on the enemy's airfields resumed as the Allied ground forces closed in on the heartland of the Reich. Then, because the Luftwaffe was short of fuel and trained pilots, most of the big battles had been the attacks on airfields.

The policy of encouraging pilots to make strafing raids by allowing them to count aircraft destroyed on the ground as victories, and thus enabling them to become aces, was controversial. It was also costly. Many more VIII Fighter Command pilots fell to ground fire than were lost in air-to-air combat. Most of the aces who failed to return from a mission did so because they were shot down by the deadly flak guns defending enemy airfields.

It is also likely that many pilots were killed in such attacks in their eagerness to become fighter aces. Some commanders resented this. Col Hubert 'Hub' Zemke of the 56th FG felt his men had a duty to go after the Luftwaffe on the ground, but considered that crediting ground kills to individual pilots was merely a publicity ploy by Gen Kepner, VIII Fighter Command's CO.

Some group commanders considered the value of the ground attack targets not worth the cost in men and machines, and for this reason some units did little strafing. There is also great variance in the various groups' ground scores. Some seemed to thrive on strafing while others did not. By the war's final stages there were commanders that thought strafing unnecessary. Nobody denied it was a deadly business.

One fact, though, is clear. From early in 1944, when ground attacks became VIII Fighter Command policy, to 18 April 1945, a total of 4163 enemy aircraft were destroyed on their airfields. This must rate as a major contribution towards the Allied victory in World War 2.

P-47 THUNDERBOLT STRAFERS

MAJ BOLEK 'MIKE' GLADYCH
61st FS/56th FG

Every ground-strafing mission requires a very thorough preparation. The pilot, or pilots, should be well acquainted with the geography of the general target area and the layout of the target itself. Particular attention

Maj Mike Gladych was a Polish Air Force pilot who escaped after the German invasion of his country in September 1939 in order to continue the fight. Having scored eight kills with the RAF between June 1941 and September 1943, he succeeded in getting himself 'loaned' to the USAAF when he grew tired of the lack of action he was seeing with the British. Counting 'Gabby' Gabreski as a personal friend, it was natural that Gladych should join the 56th FG, and he duly became a highly-regarded flight leader with the group's 61st FS. He claimed a further ten aerial kills and one strafing victory with the 56th in 1944 (he had previously destroyed seven aircraft on the ground with the RAF). Typical of contemporary Polish pilots, Gladych nursed a deep hatred of the enemy. Some of his compatriots would not claim an aircraft destroyed unless they knew the pilot had been killed

Servicing activity at Boxted on 9 November 1944 is centred around Mike Gladych's assigned P-47D 44-19718. This aircraft had disruptive pattern camouflage in two shades of dark grey on the uppersurfaces, light sky blue undersurfaces and red fuselage code letters. His 'scoreboard' featured 18 bold crosses for aerial victories and eight dull crosses for aircraft destroyed by strafing (*via Roger Freeman*)

should be paid to the location of AA guns. Pilots must memorise the best landmarks within at least five miles of the target, then choose and study best routes of approach and getaway.

Landfall should be made at approximately 15,000 ft. That altitude is to be maintained all the way to the target area. The leader locates the target, and still flying on his original course, begins to drop down to the deck. Once on the deck the formation turns 180 degrees before setting course on target, flights dropping into line astern in about 1000-yard intervals.

The approach is made at a normal cruising speed, particular aircraft flying as low as possible. About one mile before the target the first flight pulls up to 100 ft, corrects possible error in heading, gives full RPM and throttle and delivers the attack. Flight and element leaders concentrate on shooting up the target itself, whereas their wingmen act as 'anti-flak' aircraft, picking out the gun positions and silencing them. The following flights act similarly. Having past the target, every pilot stays on the deck until the leader of the formation gives the signal to climb.

In case of intense light flak, only one pass should be made, but should the target be undefended, the leader sets the pattern, detailing at least one flight to act as top cover. The top cover circles at least 2000 ft above the target in the opposite direction to the aircraft in the pattern, thus being able to intervene, if necessary, without delay.

ATTACKING TRAINS

Pilots should avoid attacking stationary trains. A train standing in a field with a locomotive emitting smoke and steam may be a trap, and therefore the target should be thoroughly examined by the formation leader before the attack. Even passenger trains are now defended by light guns, so the attack should be delivered at a 90-degree angle to the train in order to minimise the risk. One flight may be detailed to take care of flak cars. Once the guns are silenced, the rest of the formation should have no difficulties with destroying the train.

It seems as though all fighter pilots loved trains. Maj Paul Conger of the 56th FG caught a train in this marshalling yard, and the steam can be seen rising from the locomotive. Now is the time to shoot up the trucks and see what kind of explosions or flames result. Sometimes the sides of the German wagons fell away to expose flak crews manning either 20 mm or 40 mm guns

This is another train caught by Maj Conger, with lots of smoke coming from the wagons, but nothing yet to indicate what they are carrying. Aside from his penchant for trains, Conger also claimed 11.5 aerial kills, but no strafing victories

Five-kill aerial ace Lt Pete Pompetti blasts a He 111 during a strafing attack sometime in early 1944. Despite clearly registering hits on the German bomber, Pompetti did not even claim it as damaged when he returned to base. Indeed, the only time he officially strafed a He 111 was on 17 March 1944 at Beauvais, and he was in turn shot down by flak minutes later! The 84th FS/78th FG ace claimed two strafing kills prior to being made a PoW

AIRDROMES

Pilots should make passes alongside the hangars. Enemy aircraft are most likely to be found close to the perimeter track. An additional anti-flak flight may be detailed to shoot up the ground defences before the actual attack is delivered, as the airdromes are particularly well defended. Pilots should avoid crossing over the middle of the 'drome. Flying close to the edges of the airdrome is much safer because gun positions are usually situated there. By flying close to the guns the aircraft represents the target moving at a very high angular speed, and it is very difficult for the gunner to follow it. No more than *one* pass should be made at a defended airdrome.

What pilots really liked to find was enemy aircraft neatly lined up, because they made an easy target for a single firing pass. Yet more He 111s are seen here getting the 'Down to Earth' treatment in 1944

TROOPS

When attacking troops, pilots must remember that every German infantryman has been thoroughly trained in anti-aircraft firing from even small weapons (rifle and pistol). It is recommended to have all pilots in the flight fly abreast and open fire simultaneously.

ROAD CONVOYS

Road convoys should be approached with extreme caution. The same rules in attacking trains are applicable with road convoys. It is a good thing to remember that the most vulnerable point of a truck is the radiator and gas tank. Therefore, complete destruction is obtained by shooting low and aiming just behind the driver's cab.

Here, a column of enemy trucks has been caught in the open. The risk of strafing meant that most columns waited until night-fall to move

TEN COMMANDMENTS OF GROUND STRAFING

1. Before you make an attack be sure that there are no enemy aircraft in the vicinity.

2. Make an approach into the wind, because sound is killed.

3. Watch out for the gun positions, and remember they are difficult to spot before they open fire – study your own gun positions, as they are much the same.

4. The closer to the gun you fly, the safer you are.

5. Pick out the target, give full throttle, half-a-ring elevation, aim steadily and open fire from about 1000 yards.

6. At 300 yards cease fire and get as close to the ground as you dare. Forget about the target and concentrate on flying *only*.

7. When attacking a gun remember that you have the advantage of fire power. Concentrate on one gun at a time. Go in to kill the crew.

8. Take the initiative and strike first – don't wait for them to open fire.

9. Don't become over-confident because you are not hit in the first attack. At first the enemy gunners usually under-estimate your speed, but it doesn't take them long to spot their error.

10. Never spend all your ammunition.

Lt Col Ben Rimerman Commanding Officer 353rd FG

Ground strafing is certainly one of the most effective means of destroying any enemy equipment that is inflammable and unarmoured. In general, good targets are aircraft parked on the ground, motor and rail transport and petrol tanks. Usually, permanent airfield installations and concentrations of such targets as the above are more or less heavily defended by flak, and the problem arises of doing an effective job without getting too many holes in our own aeroplanes in the process.

Lt Col Ben Rimerman became CO of the 353th FG after Lt Col Duncan was shot down in July 1944. He missed becoming an aerial ace by just half a victory, but was credited with eight destroyed on the ground (*via Graham Cross*)

Occasionally, if there are not too many guns, the flak can be neutralised by either dropping a few 'frag' bombs amongst the gunners and gun positions, or by strafing the gun positions once they have been spotted. This, of course, makes the rest of the work much simpler. As a general rule, railroad flak, flak on water transports and flak on little-used or obscure landing grounds can usually be stopped because normally there are not many guns, and it is difficult for gunners to put up a heavy concentration.

However, a permanent German air force airdrome is usually so heavily defended that it is next to impossible to stop their flak. In attacking such an installation, surprise is almost a necessity to a successful attack. A good method of attack is a high speed approach on the deck and a sharp pull up at the edge of the field to 100 or 200 ft in order to spot targets and fire. The pilot should, after firing, remain on the deck for a mile or two until out of range of the guns. This type of approach may be made with four to eight aircraft, depending on the size of the dispersal area. It demands excellent low level navigation by the flight leaders, and a prearranged plan. Another effective approach for two aircraft at a time is a weaving dive from 5000 or 6000 ft and levelling off with high speed in position to fire at a previously selected target. The breakaway should be continued for a short distance on the deck with evasive action.

A few main points to remember are that a definite target should always be selected before the approach to the attack should be made. The target should be worth what you have to pay, meaning that it is foolish to lead a flight across a heavily defended airdrome to shoot up an old beat down Fieseler Storch if that is all you can see. Remember that the approach and breakaway may vary in a hundred different ways, but in each attack you must, at normal gun range, fly comparatively straight and hold your pipper on the target long enough to do the job you started on. For that short moment in any attack, you might as well forget flak and everything and concentrate on sighting, otherwise there is no point in carrying a lot of heavy 0.50-cal 'slugs' around in your guns all the time.

Capt Vic L Byers
351st FS/353rd FG

The primary reason for ground strafing is to knock out the Hun before he has a chance to use his weapons effectively. Therefore, when you make an attack, see that every bullet hits the target.

First select a suitable target – a parked aeroplane, freight train, tank, convoy or other mobilised traffic. Do not fool around with flak towers or gun positions unless they are in use. Your Intelligence Officer has all the latest gen on flak areas, so be sure to study the map carefully before each mission.

After spotting your target, go about your work in a business-like manner. *Plan your attack for one pass.* If, however, your judgment sees fit for a second attack, take every advantage of it. Come out of the sun if possible, and use all your skill to bring about an element of surprise. Speed is a decided advantage.

Start firing at medium range – first to discourage the enemy gunners, and second to adjust your pattern. Centre the needle and ball and do not fire in a turn. Concentrate on one target at a time, and continue firing until at point blank range.

After the firing pass on an airdrome, continue on the deck for a

Quite often, when escort missions were completed, Thunderbolt pilots would head for the deck and hit German targets – a task decidedly more hazardous than tangling with Luftwaffe fighters. Whilst hosing down a flak tower at Chartres with his eight 0.50-cal machine guns on 17 March 1944, the pilot who took this photograph with his gun camera almost shot down his element leader when the latter suddenly turned in front of him. Both men were from the 361st FG. Note how well the P-47's wide identification bands stand out from the Olive Drab camouflage (*via Michael O'Leary*)

A veteran of 113 missions and 406 hours of combat flying, Vic Byers finished the war as CO of the 353rd FG's 351st FS. Assigned to the group upon its formation in late 1942, Byers claimed 2.5 aerial and three strafing kills (*via Graham Cross*)

few miles to get out of the flak area. In other cases, do a steep chandelle to view your destruction and position yourself for another attack if necessary.

Freight or troop trains are most interesting targets. Knock out the engine on a broadside pass first, then use a ten- or fifteen-degree deflection pass to destroy the cars on a minimum number of attacks. Fire long bursts, and do your shooting methodically. Don't spray bullets all over the countryside – put them all in the target.

Concentrate on all targets. Keep the needle and ball centred. Do not fire in a turn, and put every bullet in the target. Make your breakaway positive and your efforts will produce favourable results.

Capt James N Poindexter
352nd FS/353rd FG

In writing this opinion of air-to-ground attack, I do so from the stand-point of a flight or squadron leader only. I should like to take an enemy airdrome for an example of an air-to-ground target.

It is my opinion that the briefing and planning of an attack is about two-thirds of the battle. From actual past occasions, the outcome or results of an attack have been greatly reduced in success due to haste in planning.

To do a thorough job I make every effort to see that each pilot knows all flak positions, all dispersal areas, disposition of the enemy aircraft and all the general points of importance in the immediate area of the target. The knowledge of these important points does not only aid the pilot in making an aggressive attack, but it ensures that well known saying 'I can whip anything I know or can see'.

If the mission goes according to plan, I like to see the following results – as in air-to-air combat, full advantage should be taken of the sun and cloud cover, or either, in the initial stages of the attack. The lead flight should attack from up sun in line abreast on their primary pass. The pass should be made from about 6000-8000 ft at a slight distance away from the airdrome to attain high speed and allow for 'flattening out' so as to give the pilot more time for firing. It is essential that each man know his gunsight to avoid the wasting of ammunition by spraying the area.

Another pilot who had joined the 353rd FG upon its formation in October 1942, James Poindexter was assigned to the group's 352nd FS. He had flown 111 missions and claimed seven aerial and four strafing victories by the time he was killed in a flying accident in P-51D 44-14859 on 3 January 1945. Leading the 352nd FS, and B Group of the 353rd FG as a whole, Poindexter had departed the group's Raydon home at 0920 hrs and headed for the rendezvous point, where the unit was to meet up with a formation of B-17s and escort them to Aschaffenburg, in Germany. Soon after take-off, several of Poindexter's flight mates spotted a fine mist trailing from the belly scoop of his Mustang. Steam then began to pour from the engine, and the pilot turned back to base. However, his vision was obscured by the coolant leak, and he hit the ground whilst trying to force-land at Capel St Mary (*via Graham Cross*)

I think it is of general opinion that 'anything burnable will burn' if hit squarely by eight 'fifties'. This fact alone should cause each pilot to concentrate on one target at a time.

In pulling away from a target I think it wise to stay low, 50 ft to 0 ft, and to make a very fast steep turn. This turn is the best possible means of avoiding flak or enemy fighters that might be working in your area. I should like to add that on either the approach or breakaway from the target, 'jinking' is good to avoid both heavy and light flak.

The above described encounter is *always* covered from *above* by *one or more* flights of the squadron, and each flight in turn supports the next flight by pulling up and giving high cover. This factor of high cover greatly assists a pilot in shooting. It allows him time to concentrate and fire on his target without a thought of an attack from the rear.

Attacks on targets of opportunity, such as motor convoys, trains, marshalling yards, etc., follow more or less much the same plan of an airdrome attack. However, the immediate situation determines the method and manner of attacking. The best way to attack these targets of opportunity is determined by the results of the first passes. Visual observation will show flak disposition and the best avenues for break-away. After these are established and known to the members of a flight or squadron, a regular ground gunnery pattern may be set up on targets such as a motor convoy or concentration of rail traffic, ensuring destruction of the entire unit. I have found it very helpful to have the squadron or flight leader pay particular attention to the AA defences of the target and deal with them first. At any rate, this sounds good – doesn't it?

I have found that while firing on any target, the best results are obtained from a long steady burst of fire. The pilot should have his aircraft properly trimmed, and should know that his sight should fire at correct range, thereby putting more bullets into the target while on it. Although this sounds as 'it says so in the book', it is still very true, and if thought out and planned by the pilot, his strafing missions will be successful.

In conclusion, I wish to say that all air-to-ground attacks should be done with one eye looking to the rear, because the Hun can't shoot you down if you can see him.

1LT HORACE Q WAGGONER 352nd FS/353rd FG

I wish to make it clear that what I am about to put down is from the point of view of a Flight Leader. However, I think that some of the things I will say may be of help to Squadron and Group Leaders as well.

There are no steadfast rules to be followed when a target has been sighted. The following is an attempt to bring out those factors of most importance.

Some care should be taken by pilots while not flying to make a study of concentrations of flak. All pilots should look over the area expected to be covered on a particular mission shortly before they take off. A good idea of areas from which to expect flak, what airfields are exceptionally dangerous, and the general areas comparatively free comes in very handy when actually on a mission.

Airfields are the most difficult and dangerous of ground targets. But if an attack is made systematically, it can be both profitable and interesting. When an airdrome is sighted and circumstances, such as type of mission, amount of gas, etc., permit an attack, first make sure that it is a worthwhile target. Look for aircraft, check their position on the field and judge from which direction the most effective pass can be made on them, always remembering the sun or possible cloud cover. Then estimate the position of the flak. Do you see emplacements? Is there a town nearby that it might be best to steer clear of? Those two factors – position of aircraft on the field and possible flak positions – determine primarily the direction of the first pass.

The initial pass on any field should be made from an altitude of from 6000 to 8000 ft. Come out of

Horace Waggoner joined the 353rd FG's 352nd FS in March 1944, and he proceeded to fly 104 missions (492 combat hours) up to VE-Day. He downed single Bf 109s on 24 and 25 December 1944, and 'made ace' with the destruction of two Fw 190s and a Bf 109 over Ruhland on 2 March 1945. Waggoner also destroyed 7.5 aircraft on the ground, with four of these being claimed on 17 April 1945 during the 353rd FG's attack on Ganacker airfield (*via Graham Cross*)

the sun or through a cloud if possible, aiming at a point just short of the field to you. Have a target picked out as you go down – an aeroplane, a hanger or gun position. Level out as you approach the deck so that you will pass over the field and approach the target at an altitude of from 50 to 75 ft. This will give you a chance to carry on to your target with plenty of room for firing. At the same time, your chance of being hit is very slight as a result of your speed. For gun positions or large targets, such as hangars, you can start firing early. In fact, in the case of gun positions, it is imperative that you start firing early. Above all, know your gun sight, and do not spray the area.

For the getaway stay *flat* on the deck till clear of the field a half to a full mile, then pull up and climb back to 6000 to 8000 ft for another pass. Be careful to pull up away from possible flak positions such as towns, barracks areas etc. On the initial pass one man, preferably the Flight Leader, should pull up early and look for flak. This will give him a basis for his decision whether to go back or not.

An airfield should not be attacked line abreast, nor should the approach be made on the deck. A diving attack as outlined above made by elements of two following each other closely is best. The wingman should be just far enough away from the leader, well up, so as to be able to make an individual pass on the target. If four ships attack at the same time, they should be in elements of two, and attacking two separate parts of the field.

For attacking trains, and here is a place for one steadfast rule, always take the engine first from 90 degrees. This gives you a chance to look over the train and see if it is to be thoroughly beaten up or left alone. Nos 1 and 2 in the flight should be able to take care of the engine, leaving Nos 3 and 4 ready to strafe the length of the train if it looks profitable.

Attacking trucks is variable, so much so that I might say take them as they come. However, a good idea is to make the primary pass from 90 degrees, watching for possible flak. Again, it is important to know your sight – you might need those wasted bullets later on.

In conclusion, I would like to say that the best possible team for strafing is a section of eight – one flight up and one flight down. Whenever you find yourself on the deck, always, if at all possible, keep a flight or element up. At any rate, always have half an eye above and behind you.

Capt Leslie P Cles
352nd FS/353rd FG

In the present stage of aerial warfare, air-to-ground firing has reached a high stage of importance. This is recognised as a deadly and important weapon. With fighters you can penetrate far behind the front and create havoc in the enemy's lines of supply and communications. You can so delay his reinforcements that major ground battles will become crushing Allied victories.

You as a pilot, however, must make every effort to ensure that your missions fulfil the highest expectations. To do this you must attack every ground target with all the knowledge that you and your fellow pilots have acquired. This can only be done if you plan and, above all, think. Never will a half-hearted pass be accepted as a substitute for an aggressive and well co-ordinated attack against the enemy.

No two ground targets will be presented in exactly the same way, but they will all have most of the same problems. Give yourself a chance to plan your attack. It may only take a few seconds, or it may take longer, but do it. An experienced pilot will have a complete pass picture in mind before he goes down. He knows which way to make the pass, how steep and where to break off.

Speed on most targets means safety. Very seldom will you fire and not receive some in return. If the target is well defended, only a very fast pass should be considered at all practical. When more than one pass is to be made in the same area, you should gain sufficient altitude between each pass to give yourself a break on the next try.

You must always bear in mind that you may be able to make only one pass. Therefore, you should make every effort to make that pass 100 per cent perfect. If you can come back, then you can go on to a new target and leave behind you a row of destroyed targets to confirm your ability at ground firing.

Leslie Cles was posted to the 353rd FG's 352nd FS in December 1942, and he had flown 101 missions in the ETO by the time he was brought down by flak on 8 November 1944 whilst attacking Plantlunne airfield. Although unable to claim a single aerial kill, Cles was credited with 6.5 strafing victories (*via Graham Cross*)

On many targets such as airfields, you can usually expect a concentration of light flak guns. Here, you will find it is never wise to rush in on your attack. Decide which side you should approach your target, picking a good one in respect to its own value and position on the field. At times, it will be much better to select or pick a less important target if it offers more safety from ground fire. Never in a strongly defended area, such as an airfield, should you start a pass without first picking your target. Don't depend on finding one on the way down. Chances are you won't find one, so it just isn't worth it.

If you find a train in a station, a couple of circles may bring it out in the open country. Here you can count on less flak, and usually a clear run. Bear in mind that trains often carry their own flak guns. These should be silenced first, if you know their position. To do this, it is advisable for No 1 to strafe the length of the train, concentrating on the flak positions. No 2 makes a coordinated 90-degree attack on the engine.

In a truck convoy, size it up for types of trucks, and what defence it carries. Most of the enemy's trucks and half-tracks carry their own supply of gasoline. If you can explode this, you will destroy your truck. Don't waste your fire on the gun that a half-track might be pulling. Hit the truck. An immobile gun is useless on the roadside. When the truck convoy has its own anti-aircraft defences, it may be safer to work in from the ends. Indeed, I have found on many occasions that you can see your truck only by coming straight down the road at it.

As much care should be taken in the approach to a ground target as you give your landing approach. When landing an aircraft, you don't come screaming down from any altitude, angle or direction. Neither do you in strafing ground targets. It is always a good idea to set up some sort of a base leg if possible. This may be very flexible, varying from one to several thousand feet, and as close to the target as the occasion demands. From this base leg the pilot can make his firing pass by doing a manoeuvre which he is proficient in – a diving turn.

One of the greatest failures in what should have been a successful attack is that the pilot made his approach too steep or too shallow. Both give almost the same results. That is, your mind is half occupied with the fear of hitting something with your aeroplane, rather than full concentration being placed on the target. When you are too steep, the tendency is to open fire at long range and stop firing at your best range. If the pass, however, is too low, the tendency is to fire short, snap bursts which are very ineffective. You always have to pull up to avoid some object, when could be doing your best firing. A good pass on most targets will be one that is as low as a good safety margin will allow. This will clear the aeroplane of all ground obstacles, and give the best possible allowance for the pull out. The fire can be held to a close and deadly range.

If possible, always start your dive from several thousand feet, and close to the target. Set a base leg from this position, and do not dive straight to the target. If you do, your dive will be too steep, leaving you a sitting duck for flak. Go down steep on your base and you will gain plenty of speed. Then, by being close to the target, you will not lose your speed in a long, fast firing run. Plan your dive so that when you turn on the target, you will also shallow the dive for the best firing run. Remember to make a long, steep dive, followed by a short and shallower firing run. Make full use of the sun and cloud conditions. Diving from the sun, or from behind a cloud, can hide your approach until you are almost on the target. If you are firing on a flak position, a steeper dive and greater opening range is considered better.

The return fire may be heavy enough to make it advisable to use evasive action in all but the last part of your dive. Slight pumping of the stick and small turns will throw the ground gunners off your flight path. Skidding is useless. A ground gunner at a few thousand feet can't see if you are skidding or not, so you won't fool him. On the pass, evasive action can be carried only so far. When you line your sight up on the target, forget the flak until you are through firing. If you can't do this, don't go down. When you start firing, don't forget everything you've ever learned. It's still ground gunnery, but this time you have a better target. By closing to less than 500 yards to fire, you will run up against this.

You are doing about 400 mph, which will give you about a 2.7-second burst from 500 yards to the target. You may need all this to get your target. It is not good enough to just hit anywhere on the target. Almost every type of target will have a more vulnerable area somewhere on it. Know these areas and aim for them.

When sighting, use a little thought as to where your sighting point will be. Your guns are bore sighted for around 300 yards. Therefore, there will be more bullet drop in the opening ranges. You are also travelling at a speed in which the angle of attack will be on the negative side. These combined factors will require more than the usual amount of sight elevation. The sight will have to be placed at least on top of the target, and in some cases even slightly higher. The 'G' pull on the bullet stream in a turn will require additional lead if you must fire in a turn. This, however, should be avoided if possible.

When the range is correct and you are on the target, then fire a good steady burst. You won't have time to take several short bursts. Neither will you be able to fire, see where your bullets go, and fire again. You must use, and trust, your sight. Then make full use of the few seconds you have.

Never spray bullets around – pick one target and hold it. One destroyed target is far better than several damaged. Then, when you are no longer on the target, stop firing. It's a pure waste of expensive ammunition to keep on firing as you pull out. If you are fortunate to have an undefended target, set up a flying school gunnery pattern and go to it, but make your passes count.

The breakaway will depend on the target and the location. If there is very little or no flak, a climbing turn is good, as it is easy to reform on and results can better be observed. When you encounter heavy opposition from ground fire, keep low on the breakaway. They can't hit you if they can't see you. Fly in the tree-tops and weave until you are well clear of the area. The lower the better. When you do pull up, look around, clear your tail and make sure that you are not pulling up over a gun battery.

If a wingman can not find a target when his leader goes down, he can follow to a few thousand feet and pick up the leader on the other side of the target. The wingman should make every effort though to coordinate the attack with his leader, and make good use of the guns he carries.

There will be times when it is advisable to send only one ship down. The rest of the flight should drop down low enough to provide adequate top cover, and then pick up the leader as he comes off the target. Some ships can also be used as a diversion to the main attack. There will always be exceptions to the procedures described here.

The same general principles that were first learned in ground gunnery apply here. It is only a matter of using your head in picking and destroying the target.

MAJ KENNETH W GALLUP
350th FS/353rd FG

Most of our ground gunnery has not been to a definitely briefed plan, but has more or less been carried on in the manner of 'after completing our mission with the "Big Friends", we will drop down on the deck and shoot up targets of opportunity'. Our briefing would usually consist of information regarding the general distribution of flak and enemy weapons in our particular area, and possibly some data on what we might find in the vicinity in the way of trains, convoys, airdromes and so forth.

In areas where there is very little flak, or ground fire, I have found it best to stay up at around 4000 ft, and believe that this altitude has several distinct advantages. By maintaining this altitude, I find that I have an

A pre-war pilot with the USAAC, Ken Gallup had served with the 37th Pursuit Group and the 36th FG in both the Panama Canal Zone and the USA, before moving to the ETO with the latter group in the spring of 1944. CO of the P-47-equipped 53rd FS, he transferred to the 353rd FG in May 1944. Initially serving with the group HQ flight, Gallup was made CO of the 350th FS the following month. He remained in command until November of that year, when he returned to the HQ flight. Gallup would fly 70 missions with the 353rd, claiming nine aerial and two strafing kills between 28 May and 12 August 1944 (*via Graham Cross*)

excellent view of the countryside, and am able to see far enough in front of my flight path to avoid any heavily defended areas, such as the larger towns and airdromes. This not only enables me to study a particular target long enough to decide its worth, but also affords ample time to plan my attack.

A few thousand feet above the terrain gives more protection for the pilot by making it possible to 'get the hell out in a hurry' if a big concentration of ground fire is encountered. In addition, I am in a position to trim my ship for the higher speed caused by the diving pass, and at the same time make a good steep approach, which gives an extremely heavy concentration of bullets in one spot. After the initial pass, a regular gunnery pattern can be established around the target, or the targets, as the case may be, and the more important ones picked out and destroyed. Of course, this system may have its disadvantages, but as far as creating the greatest amount of damage to the enemy in a few minutes time, it seems to work very well.

In heavily defended areas, the element of surprise is one of the most important factors to be considered. Personally, I like to come in on the deck at a very high speed and bounce up just high enough before I get to the target so that I will be able to make a good pass at it, and yet not too high so as to offer a good target for the defending gunners. Then, I bounce down to the deck again and get away before the enemy is able to get well organised. Good navigation for this type of pass is essential, however, and a prominent landmark, preferably very close to the target, should be selected while the pilot has altitude. To get the most out of the element of surprise it is necessary to stay right on the deck till the last possible second.

Another ground gunnery approach which has worked out satisfactorily in the past is to come in at about 8000 ft, make a steep dive on the target, coming in fast and low, then convert the additional speed back into altitude, and if the ground fire is not too intense, bounce back down on the target again in the same manner and so on. During the time of the initial dive, or let down, I trim my ship for the excess speed, but at the same time keep twisting and turning from left to right in order to make a more difficult target out of myself. This type of approach and procedure is done without the element of surprise, but the swiftness of the attack often makes up for this.

Regardless of what type of procedure is used, or what type of target is being attacked, I try to keep in mind that 'this is going to be a good approach and that I'm going to make every move and every bullet count, as it might be the only approach, and the only opportunity, that I will get to make at this particular target'.

P-38 LIGHTNING STRAFERS

COL ROY W OSBORN
COMMANDING OFFICER
364th FG

The views expressed herein are representative not of myself alone but of the entire group. We have been engaged in ground strafing and low level bombing since this Command began that type of operation. Our record of aircraft destroyed on the ground is not large compared to that of most groups. However, we have been on the deck anywhere from the Berlin area back to this side of Paris.

Perhaps it might be interesting to compare two of our 'Jackpot' missions, which had as their objective the destruction on the ground of enemy aircraft, locomotives, and targets of military importance. On the first, flown on 15 April, we lost seven P-38s and claimed four enemy aircraft, of which only two were on the ground. On the second, on 21 May, we lost two P-38s and claimed twenty enemy aircraft destroyed. The first mission was in the Bremen, Hamburg, Stade area, and the second in the Muritz Lake area north of Berlin. If we can analyse these two missions and learn something from them, we can be better prepared for future operations of this type.

On 15 April we were a new group, having gone operational the month before. We were inexperienced not only in ground strafing, but in all our operations. On that day we managed to get through some bad weather and

Well-worn Olive Drab and Neutral Gray P-38Js of the 383rd FS/364th FG rendezvous with the bombers over a typically cloudy East Anglia in the late spring of 1944. Based at Honington from February 1944 through to war's end, the 383rd marked its Lightnings both with the code N2 and a large white circle – the latter unfortunately obscuring the serial number. The factory construction number is, however, still carried on the nose of the P-38 closest to the camera. The 364th FG claimed 191 aircraft destroyed on the ground, 80 of which were credited to the 383rd FS, making it the most successful strafing unit in the group. The 364th FG as a whole achieved 24 strafing victories with the P-38 between 29 March and 24 May 1944 (*via Michael O'Leary*)

into our assigned area. There, the whole group hit the deck and began shooting up everything in sight. Flak was generally bad over the whole area. In addition, flights became widely separated and navigation of some misfired, and they found themselves over the outskirts of large, well defended cities such as Hamburg and Bremen. Airfields were crossed haphazardly, and in most cases there were no aircraft as targets, only light flak positions throwing a withering fire at us. Eventually, with flights and elements scattered, the group withdrew, some back up through the clouds, some on the deck over the North Sea. Because of the weather, only 36 P-38s reached the assigned area. Out of the 36, 23 were hit by light flak, seven of them being lost.

On 21 May the group was again despatched on a low level mission into Germany. Contact with the deck was made north of Berlin in the Muritz Lake area. Here, all resemblance to the former mission ended. The group was by necessity split down to squadrons, but no squadron was completely broken down. None of our aircraft dropped below 6000 ft unless there was an excellent, worthwhile target. Areas likely to hold flak were avoided simply because they could be seen in time. Top cover was maintained all the time, and flights on top 'cued' the deck flight into airdromes. Advantage was taken of the sun and of all geographical factors on every pass, instead of sweeping always in one direction. The group withdrew very nearly intact. We had seven aircraft battle damaged and two lost – claims were for twenty destroyed. These aircraft were destroyed on six airfields across the heart of Germany.

Let me stress above all that none of our flights went down on an objective that was not worth the risk of a P-38 and its pilot. This, in my opinion, is the most important lesson we can learn about ground attack. All leaders should constantly be aware of this problem. A questionable target that offers only a small chance for success should be abandoned. It is a hard lesson to learn, but I believe most groups in VIII Fighter Command have learned it. We learned it the hard way on 15 April and again a month or so later. On that day over France, a flight went down to strafe an airfield. No aircraft were visible, but the attack was made anyhow. Out of the four aircraft attacking, three were lost, including the flight commander, and the fourth was badly shot up and came home on one engine. There were no claims – there had been no target to warrant the attack.

It would require too much writing on my part, and too much reading on yours, to mention all the ideas that we have here in the 364th on how to attack specific or general targets. There must be good leadership within the squadrons and flights, common sense on the part of all and sound briefing prior to the mission. Above all, there must be a 'down to earth' sense of value in regard to targets to be attacked, and losses to be risked.

Having converted to P-51 Mustangs, the 364th FG rids itself of a damaged Lightning, which is destined never to be repaired. This 'bellied in' P-38J was photographed at Honington on 23 July 1944 while being broken up for spares, which were in turn passed on to the Ninth Air Force. Here, a 467th Service Squadron hangar crew are removing an outer wing section. A trace of the 364th's white identification marking can be seen at the bottom/front of the engine cowling. Note the narrow black backing line to the marking, this being a regular feature when the white marking was applied to a 'silver' finish aircraft. At least five locomotive silhouettes can also be seen on the nose of the P-38, denoting that its pilot was something of a 'train-busting' specialist (*via John Stanaway*)

P-51 MUSTANG STRAFERS

COL DONALD J M BLAKESLEE
COMMANDING OFFICER
4th FG

AIRDROMES

Surprise, speed and a variation of the attack – these are the things to keep in mind when strafing a Hun airdrome.

I consider surprise to be one of the chief factors in a successful strafe. When my group is assigned to strafe a particular target, I ask for all the photographs available. I want to know what the airdrome looks like before I get there. I want my intelligence officer to get the best information he can on the defence, and to pin-point the positions of flak posts if possible. I want to know what kind, and how many, aircraft are reported to be on the field, and just where on the field I can expect to find them parked. I want to know what the terrain around the airdrome is.

Col Don Blakeslee was CO of the 4th FG from January to November 1944, during which time he planned and flew on many of the group's early strafing missions. Blakeslee was a no-nonsense leader whose unit's success was due to his pilots being well-disciplined and highly-motivated. He also led many of the initial missions flown by the Eighth Air Force's new groups. Blakeslee's final wartime tally was 14.5 aerial (three with the RAF) and 1.5 strafing kills. Note how the official censor has blanked out the background of this photograph, taken at Debden in early 1944

One of Don Blakeslee's most successful pilots, John Godfrey reputedly had the 'sharpest' eyes in the 4th FG, which goes a long way to explaining his success in action in 1943-44. Aside from his aerial kills, he was also credited with the destruction of 13.67 aircraft on the ground. And like most VIII Fighter Command aces brought down in action, it was Godfrey's passion for strafing that would prove his downfall. However, he was not hit by flak in his P-51D on 24 August 1944. Instead, his fighter was terminally damaged by machine gun fire from his wingman, fellow strafing ace Lt Melvin Dickey – it was not until he returned from captivity that he learned who had shot him down! Godfrey had destroyed four Ju 52/3ms at an airfield at Nordhausen just prior to his untimely demise. Dickey also enjoyed success on this day, claiming three Junkers transports (but not Godfrey's Mustang!). Godfrey was always better known as the partner of Don Gentile in their many aerial combats, but he participated in many strafing missions, and led some too. In the month before he was shot down, Godfrey destroyed seven enemy aircraft on the ground. His final score was 16.333 aerial and 13.67 strafing victories (*via Sam Sox*)

With all this information to hand I can plan the approach best calculated to achieve surprise. I use terrain – hills, gulleys and trees – for cover, and such airdrome installations as hangars, etc., to screen my approach. I never come right in on an airdrome if I can help it. If I have planned to attack an airdrome beforehand, I pick an initial point (IP) some ten miles away – some easily recognisable place. I have my course from there to the 'drome worked out. Once in the air, I take my boys right past the airdrome as if I had no intention of attacking it at all. At my IP, I let down and swing back flat on the deck. I usually try and have another check-point on the course from my IP not far from the airdrome, and when I pass that I know I am definitely coming in on the right field. I don't like to end up on an airdrome before I realise I am even coming to one. But once I hit the 'drome, I really get down on the deck. I don't mean five feet up – I mean so low that the grass is brushing the bottom of the scoop.

For a squadron attack on a Hun airfield, I do not recommend sending sections in waves. This is a good way to get half the outfit shot down. In my own group, I want as many as eight in at one time, if possible. These should be well abreast and, knowing our target beforehand, we go right in full bore in a straight line. Once you start an attack of this kind, don't turn or swerve. If you do, there is a danger of collision, or entering another man's pattern of fire.

103

I plan on making only one pass on an airdrome, and after my first pass, I climb to about 3000 or 4000 ft – well beyond the field – and circle and look back to observe the damage in the form of smoke or fire. I see where the rest of the boys are, and call upon the R/T and ask how the flak was. If there wasn't too much on the first pass, and I figure we can afford to have a go a second time, we line up and repeat the performance. This time I usually leave eight aircraft up for top cover. These should be at 4000 or 5000 ft – well beyond the range of small arms fire. On the first pass I never bother with top cover, as we are all on the deck, and any Hun that wants to bounce us is welcome to try.

After the attack on the field, stay on the deck for a good mile beyond the 'drome before pulling up. The break should consist of rudder yawing. Never cock a wing up. If you must turn on the 'drome, do flat skidding turns. Don't give the Hun a better target to shoot at.

I prefer to get down low and shoot up at any aircraft on the ground, rather than come in high and shoot down. Usually, I fire a short burst from long range and correct for it as I come in.

My method of attacking an unassigned airfield – a target of opportunity, one I have noticed on the way back – is about the same. The only difference is that in one case I have quite a lot of information beforehand, and in the other I have to get a mental picture of the field. I watch for the location of aircraft and dispersals, as well as any guns firing, all in the few seconds it takes to fly by. Once I decide to attack, my method is the same.

Flying a decidedly non-tactical formation, three P-51Ds from the 4th FG's 335th FS pull in tight to the camera aircraft in August 1944. Leading the three-ship in WD-C is Col Don Blakeslee, and his wingmen are Capts Bob Church (WD-A) and Bob Manie (WD-I)

It's important to go in full bore. You want all the speed you can muster. The aircraft should be trimmed for high speed before you go in, and not for the cruising speed at which you go by your home field.

Vary the plan of your attacks, if possible. If the Hun doesn't know what to expect, the chances are you'll get away with it a lot easier. You can't use the same plan twice. Achieve surprise.

Surprise had much to do with the most successful strafing attack this group ever made on a Hun airdrome. On 5 April 1944, the outfit strafed four airdromes deep in Germany, and claimed 45 aircraft destroyed and 49 damaged on the ground. These claims were later raised by the assessing authorities to 50 destroyed. The airdromes were Brandenburg/Briest, Brandenburg/Industriehafen, Weissewarte/Buch and Stendal, none of which were more than 40 miles from Berlin. That day we had been assigned to attack Jüterbog airdrome, but were unable to find it because of overcast conditions. My intelligence officer had provided gen on large concentrations of enemy aircraft on the fields named, and we found them easily. We attacked in the manner I have described.

My point in bringing this attack up is to emphasise that it was surprise, not tactics or a particular method, that allowed us to do as well as we did. These Hun airdromes were well inland, and at that phase of the war the Jerry must have felt rather secure in there. They had never been strafed before – perhaps they never expected to be. At any rate, they were surprised completely. At Stendal, there was no flak at all on our first three passes, and only meagre flak on our fourth. There, we destroyed 23 German aircraft and damaged 14 more. But the same operation could not be pulled with the same success today. The Jerry has learned, and we must change.

TARGETS OTHER THAN AIRDROMES

Barges – I do not consider these worthwhile targets unless intelligence information indicates they are explosive targets. Machine gun fire on barges is rather ineffective as far as I am concerned.

Other attractive targets for fighter pilots in occupied Europe were canal barges, which were usually loaded with freight. Don Blakeslee did not rate barges as priority strafing targets

Before any fighter unit set up a pattern to strafe an airfield, one flight usually went down to silence the defences. This flak tower, on the edge of a field, is just coming under fire

Lt Ralph 'Kid' Hofer was described by Col Don Blakeslee as 'unmanageable'. Nevertheless, he became one of the 4th FG's top aces, but it was almost impossible for him to keep his allocated station in formation. He not only ran up a score of 15 aerial victories, but destroyed another 12 on the ground, most of which were scored at the end of May 1944. One of the most flamboyant characters to fly with VIII Fighter Command, Hofer had joined the Royal Canadian Air Force prior to America's entry into the war. He was amongst the first 4th FG pilots to 'make ace' with the Mustang in the ETO, scoring six of his eventual fifteen kills in this particular P-51B-15 (42-106924), which he named *Salem Representative* in honour of his home town in Missouri. He is seen here with the 334th FS's orphan dog 'Duke', which adopted Hofer. Note his non-regulation long hair and lucky college football jersey, which he religiously wore on every sortie. This official USAAF photograph was taken at Debden on 14 May 1944. Killed on 2 July 1944, details of Hofer's final demise have only recently emerged. He was shot down by flak whilst making a lone strafing attack on an airfield in Yugoslavia (*via Dick Martin*)

Flak Towers – I personally would not deliberately pick one for a target, except if it were in my way. A flak tower that is not firing is probably not in use, and there is no sense in attacking it anyway.

Convoys, Trains, etc. – My methods are about the same. I usually let down to about 2000 or 3000 ft and cruise around looking for targets. When I find one, I get directly over it and go down in a 20- to 30-degree dive. I feel this enables me to concentrate my fire. The attack would be varied if the convoy was in a gully or behind trees.

BOMBING WITH FIGHTER AIRCRAFT

Results achieved in fighter-bombing are generally good. There is a need for practice, however, in order to obtain greater accuracy. On buildings, locos, etc., an average pilot can do a fairly good job. Flat targets such as tracks need more practised men. I advocate dive-bombing on flat and heavily defended targets and glide-bombing on buildings and bridges.

I have no particular method of bomb aiming. I go down in a steep glide from 3000 ft, and when I am so low I think I am going to hit the deck, let the bombs go, then pull up and turn off to one side, never ahead. I have tried dropping belly tanks filled with gasoline and then strafing them to set targets afire, but to my mind it is not too successful. The trouble is the tanks fall different ways – some tumble backwards, while others go straight down. You can't count on them.

When attacking bridges, I prefer to carry the heaviest bomb available. My plan is to hit the embankment or approach, leaving the span alone. On bridge attacks I favour glide bombing in a 30-degree angle.

In general, my pilots and I realise ground strafing involves a greater risk than shooting Huns down in the air. But it seems to be quite as important. Besides, we get more fun out of strafing ground targets instead of airfields – no one really likes to attack the latter.

Concluding, I want to say a word about tactics. My feeling is that there is entirely too much emphasis placed on methods of strafing and on so-called tactics. Strafing is a simple process. You pick a target and shoot it up. As long as you are comfortable and get away with it, that's all there is to it. Every pilot probably has a different idea on how to do it. A general rule just can't be laid down, for one method is probably no better than another.

COL JOHN B HENRY JR
COMMANDING OFFICER
339th FG

The ground strafing tactics of this organisation are based on the principle that maximum damage to ground installations must be accomplished in the shortest possible time, during which our aeroplanes are within the range of light flak. Because of the extreme vulnerability of the P-51 to any kind of damage, it is considered by most of our pilots that attacks on ground targets are not worth the risk unless those targets are poorly defended, and are extremely vulnerable to 0.50-cal machine gun fire.

Most of our ground strafing objectives are targets of opportunity, and tactics are varied somewhat to suit the circumstances of the attack. It is considered that good air discipline and a solid understanding of the basic principles of strafing are the most important explanations of our light losses while 'on the deck'.

While searching for the targets we prefer to cruise at from 12,000 to 14,000 ft, with all flights line abreast. When a desirable target is called in, a squadron splits into two sections. One section conducts the attack while the other provides the air cover. The first pass across the target is made at a speed of about 400 mph if there is reason to suppose that ground fire will be encountered.

Flights making the attack are spread astern at intervals of 3000 ft or more. This interval is large enough to allow each man in the flight to pick out his target and study it before opening fire. The interval is also large enough to prevent any damage being inflicted on preceding flights by ricochets, and to allow the attack to be broken off at any moment. Men flying astern always cover the flights which have immediately preceded them across the target in an effort to reduce the ground fire when it is encountered, but flights not already committed to attack breakaway as soon as flak is called in and the order has been passed out by the squadron leader.

Most of our ground strafing has been done by individual squadrons acting independently. However, when two or more squadrons are acting together, one squadron is always left for top cover.

Flights in trail, with individual aeroplanes flying several hundred feet apart, is the preferred formation for ground strafing. However, when the target does not have sufficient horizontal length, we often break off into two-ship elements. For dive-bombing, we usually use a string formation of individual aeroplanes. Each pilot must be allowed to give his entire effort toward gaining the utmost accuracy, whether it is in firing the guns or dropping a bomb. The interval between aeroplanes is large enough so that no attention need be given toward avoiding a collision.

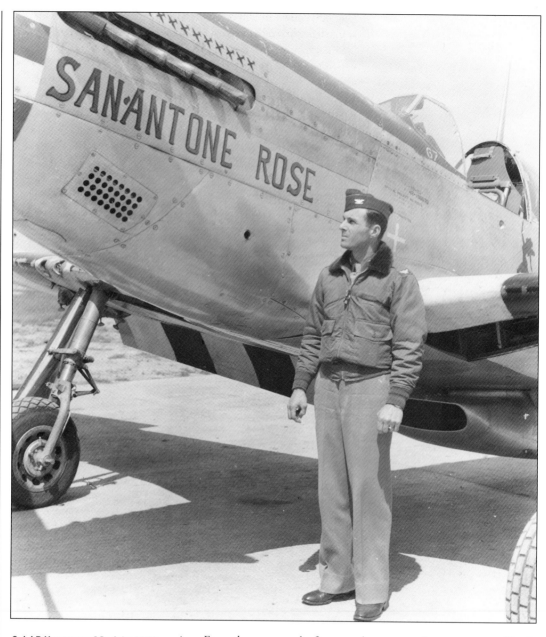

Col J B Henry was CO of the 339th FG during its entire combat career. Although the group did not reach the frontline until 30 April 1944, the 339th became well-known for its outstanding combat record in the air and on the ground. Many of its pilots were numbered among the Eighth Air Force's list of high-scoring strafing aces. The group also achieved success against a variety of ground targets. By the end of the war, the 339th had been credited with 235 aerial victories, plus an amazing 440 on the ground

From the moment the first aeroplane crosses the target, every effort is made to keep waves of flights on the target without interruption until satisfactory damage has been done, flak has been called in, or until all but a reserve of ammunition has been expended. On some targets the top cover has been called in to make a few attacks, and the flights that are low on ammunition replace them.

A very strong effort has been made to get pilots 'accuracy conscious' in ground strafing. Motion pictures showed the typical burst starting a few hundred fee in front of the target and crossing through the target to a few hundred feet on the other side, without a pause.

At present, we usually try to fire one or two 'sighting-in' bursts at long range so that at 1200 ft or so the pilot can be all set to open up with the long burst down to 500 or 600 ft without a break. Pilots were told to apply slight forward pressure to the stick during the entire pass to correct for bullet drop, and to cease firing the moment their sights went off the target. The advice worked so well that recently one squadron of 14 aeroplanes set fire to 16 German aircraft on a field and also destroyed two gliders. Despite seeing much action, most of the ships had a small reserve of ammunition to come home on.

Yet even on this job a lot of ammunition was wasted by firing into aeroplanes already burning, and by making multiple passes on the gliders. Some of this waste could just as well have been expended in the fixed installations of the field. Unmanned gun positions were sighted and called in but, by keeping aeroplanes on the attack at all times, these positions were already covered. Top cover of this attack was a flight of four and two stragglers from another group. They patrolled the outskirts of the field.

It is all good and well to say that one pass is enough for any airfield, but we find that 400 mph is too fast to inflict any great damage in one pass. So, unless ground fire has been encountered, before the last flight passes, we have the first flight in position for another attack. After the first pass the flights start coming in from different directions, but always remain in mutual support of each other. The pattern is at a very low altitude.

After a long lull, when no opposition has been encountered from the Luftwaffe in the air, a couple of missions of ground strafing, despite the risk, does a lot for the morale of the pilots. Just to fire their guns and to know they are back to the job of doing some damage to the enemy boosts their spirits, tiding them over until the next batch of Jerries comes to meet us in the air.

By flying past a ground target after it has been called in, we are usually able to position ourselves for the attack, either out of the sun or down-wind. In the late afternoon, when the sun is low on the horizon, we prefer the 'out-of-sun' attack if the ground defences are unknown. However, for the most part, we try to attack downwind so the smoke from the target will not obstruct the vision of the pilots following.

Crosswind targets are avoided when possible because of the excessive drift which sets in during the long burst. Incidentally, these long bursts are almost a 'must' since most of our aeroplanes have only four guns, and usually at least one or two of them are jammed and useless. One of our 'pet peeves' against this aeroplane is its lack of firepower in combat models prior to the D-series.

Briefing for ground strafing missions has been of very little value, as the information we receive on the nature of the target, and its defences, has never proven to be correct. When ordered on a ground-strafing mission, it would be of great value to know the location of light flak positions and heavy flak positions within a radius of 50 miles. By knowing where the heavy flak positions are in the area, we could ascertain the best course to take in climbing back up to a safe altitude. As it is we usually leave the target area, then climb in a series of turns to avoid cities.

During the attack, the squadron leader pulls about 40 inches of manifold pressure, and maintains the highest possible airspeed. After the first pass across the target, 250 to 300 mph is considered desirable, and for climbing back to altitude, about 200 mph.

In summary, the following five points are considered of chief importance in keeping losses low whilst inflicting a maximum amount of damage to ground targets.

1. Dependable air discipline.

2. Accuracy of fire to make every bullet count.

3. Keeping the target (especially airdromes) covered at all times so that gun positions cannot be manned, or if they are, they can be fired upon immediately.

4. Mutual support among all flights at all times.

5. Minimum altitude at all times, and a safe alley of retreat for climbing back to altitude after the attack is completed.

COL JOE L MASON
COMMANDING OFFICER
352nd FG

GROUND ATTACKS ON AN AIRDROME

When the mission calls for shooting up a specific airdrome, you should obtain all the information available about the target – flak maps and photos – and look at it on all scales of maps. You should know what you are going to shoot at before you shoot, if it's possible to know. Certain flights should be assigned certain targets on the field to be hit at certain times. This sort of planned attack works nicely if everything goes according to the mission briefing. Everyone has his own idea of how this type of work should be done, and here are mine.

Firstly, we operate on a few basic fundamentals. Namely, we do not feel that losing one of our own aircraft just to destroy one enemy aircraft on the ground is a good swap. In other words, unless otherwise ordered, we will not attack an airdrome unless we know that there is plenty of stuff there to shoot at. We do not aim to pay for each victory with one loss. After we have decided the target is sufficiently juicy, we then proceed. Not knowing the amount of flak, we make an effort to split the flak as much as possible. This is done as follows, for in most cases the German knows we are around, but he doesn't know exactly what we're going to do, so we give him lots to see in the way of a diversion.

Have one squadron circle the field at 10,000 to 12,000 ft – far enough out to be poor light flak targets. While this is going on, the other two squadrons have moved off and hit the airdrome on the deck from two different directions, and only make one pass. This fundamental is simple – the German has just so many guns, so the more moving targets going through his gun range, the less chance he has in hitting any of them, and the squadron overhead making dive-bombing feints is attracting some of that attention. This plan has worked well on a number of occasions. The diversion squadron is also the top cover squadron.

GROUND ATTACK ON TRANSPORTATION

On convoys we use the same principle. We know there won't be as much flak as there is on an airdrome, so we try and make the attack from the up sun side, with a whole squadron line abreast and shooting at the same time. The second squadron behind them does the same thing, whilst the third squadron stays above the airfield providing top cover. If no return fire is encountered, then repeated attacks are made until all the vehicles are burning.

With trains, you always have the factor of a flak car being present. They can be mean. We lost two pilots to them. It depends entirely on what kind of a train you encounter as to how you handle the problem. Troop trains are juicy, but will always have one or two flak cars that must be taken care of first. Tank cars burn very nicely. We started the idea of dropping half-full wing tanks into the side of wooden freight cars and then setting the gas on fire. It works nice – the tanks split open and spill gas all over the place, which is ignited very easily by the next guy in. This form of attack is only good for targets that will burn.

GROUND SHOOTING

The greatest tendency when shooting at targets on the ground is to waste bullets. When making an airdrome one pass attack, I think it's okay to start shooting way back, and to continue shooting all the way through. You might waste bullets, but all these bullets flying around slightly disrupts the ground fire that is shooting back at you and the other guys in the squadron.

With trains and convoys where you encounter no return fire, you must make every bullet count. Our ammunition is belted with five rounds of tracer for every 50 rounds from the end of the belt. We have a rule that you will not shoot past that tracer on a ground target – we lost some '109s one day because not a damn soul in the group had any bullets left. And good shooting is good shooting, regardless of the target, and good shooting is what kills Germans.

Col Joe L Mason took the 352nd FG to England, and led the group until November 1944. The unit would not only become a top scorer in air-to-air combat, but was also responsible for causing much damage to the enemy on the ground. A hot-tempered leader, he often told his pilots that he was the best there was in the air

Senior men in the 352nd FG get together for a group shot at Bodney in early November 1944. They are, from left to right, Lt Col James Mayden (soon to become CO of the group), Maj Willie O Jackson (CO of the 486th FS), Maj George Preddy (CO of the 328th FS), Col Joe Mason (then CO of the group) and Lt Col John Meyer (CO of the 487th FS and soon to become Deputy CO of the group). They are posing in front of 'Red Dog' Mason's P-51D 44-14911 *THIS IS IT!*, which was the last of six fighters (two P-47Ds, two P-51Bs and two P-51Ds) that had been assigned to him during his ETO tour. Note the 487th FS badge on 'J C' Meyer's A2 flying jacket (*via* Michael O'Leary)

BOMBING WITH FIGHTER AIRCRAFT

On specific assigned targets, I think it's okay to use fighter aircraft as bombers. I'm partial to dive-bombing, as I think it's as accurate as any. Anything less than 1000 lbs is not too much good on bridges. On all the bridges we've bombed, we have only been successful in dropping one span. I'm sorry to have to admit that, but it seems to be the truth. Bombing with a fighter aircraft is 100 per cent personal skill, and it's just like playing basketball – the more you practice, the more baskets you can sink.

We in VIII Fighter Command have not had the time, ranges, or equipment to practise fighter-bombing to even approach the degree which could be obtained. But we are basically an escort outfit, and in that we have had sufficient practice to come closer to perfection. The score board shows that. You can mess up a lot of railroad by flying straight and level and dropping one bomb at a time. If done right, one group can break the tracks every half-mile for about 50 miles. That should drive the Hun nuts trying to fix it – it's not a permanent injury, but I'll bet it makes him mad as hell. A good fighter-bomber pilot can hit his target from any dive angle at any altitude – that is what takes practice.

GENERAL

When flying on a ground mission at medium and low altitudes, you are open for attack from both above and below. We fly our group that way – to get caught by the Hun from above is just dumbness. We always make one squadron responsible for the top part of the sky. They don't like it because they don't get to shoot much, unless we find so many ground targets that we swap top cover squadron in the middle of a mission after the other two have shot up their ammo. But we rotate the squadrons so they all get a crack at it.

My boys will tackle any target with pleasure if they know that, if completed the right way, we'll really help those guys on the beachhead.

A fighter pilot who doesn't want to shoot his guns is no fighter pilot. I continuously have to warn them about non-military targets – the angle they shoot so it won't kill half the French in France, etc.

The aerial photos of targets are not much good, as they are either too young or too old. But the job of supplying new photos for all fighter and bomber groups on a weekly basis would naturally be impossible. We do the best we can, and usually identify the field by surrounding landmarks.

We have not yet run into a truck convoy that was so big that one group could not handle it. The largest one was about 26 trucks – we had about 22 of them burning when the 56th FG came in and helped us finish off the rest. Incidentally, I saw no German leave any truck from the time I first spotted the convoy, and it was moving when I first saw it. There must have been a lot of dead Germans someplace.

As to shooting up barges, I think they should be shot up according to what higher command says is in them. I think they are supposed to know such things.

I do not think the boys are fully aware of the service they are rendering by these ground attacks. There is no way of assessing or scoring the damage they have done. Shooting up convoys, and especially staff cars and despatch riders, is considered great sport.

I think a good poop sheet on the effect of the fighter boys on that beachhead would be a good thing, mostly in regard to the work of VIII Fighter Command.

CAPT GORDON B COMPTON
351st FS/353rd FG

The enemy stands to lose more on the ground now than ever before, and these losses can be increased considerably by fighter personnel in their attacks on 'targets of opportunity'. In order for such attacks to be effective, however, they must be planned as far in advance as possible, and carried out in a 'balls out', aggressive manner. This is especially true of attacks on airdromes and marshalling yards, etc., which are liable to be well defended by ground fire. Targets not defended do not present much of a problem, but attacks on those which are must take advantage of the element of surprise. Also, timed attacks on a target from different directions, taking advantage of a bright sun, can confuse enemy ground fire during the initial stages of an attack – but not for long.

All the planning possible won't make an attack successful if each individual doesn't take it upon himself to put his bullets in the most effective place. Ground strafing requires firing at long ranges and at high speeds on targets which are usually stationary. Therefore, the closing speed is much faster than in air-to-air firing. Each pilot must take this into consideration, and learn to control his fire, before the enemy will suffer much from his presence in their territory.

Ranking strafing ace of the 353rd FG, Capt Gordon Compton claimed 5.5 aerial and 15 ground kills during the course of 114 missions (420 combat hours). He joined the 353rd FG's 351st FS upon the group's formation in October 1942, and remained with the unit until war's end (*via Graham Cross*)

Four aces from the 351st FS/353rd FG. They are, from left to right, Capt Frank N Emory (two aerial kills and ten on the ground), Capt William J Maguire (seven aerial kills and one on the ground), Maj Vic L Byers (2.5 aerial kills and three on the ground) and Capt Gordon B Compton (5.5 aerial kills and 15 on the ground). The aircraft behind them is Capt Compton's P-51D 44-72299 *Little Bouncer*

Lt Col William B Bailey
Commanding Officer
352nd FS/353rd FG

There are certain fundamental rules which every unit must observe in order to carry out a successful ground attack, but these rules are by now self-evident to all who lead them. The real crux of the problem, as I see it, lies in training the individual pilot to attack these targets properly, and with the desired effect. I have seen thousands of rounds of ammunition wasted by pilots who, for one reason or another, fail to hit their targets, and it is this inefficiency and waste upon which I have declared war.

The first few times a new pilot goes down on a ground target he is probably just plain scared. He feels there are hundreds of hidden guns which will open up on him at any moment. Naturally, this mental attitude will reflect on the firing accuracy of the individual concerned. He will invariably come in too fast, too high or too low, slipping and skidding without much thought of hitting the target until he is closing so fast that he has only the briefest interval to fire.

The first step in overcoming these errors is to install in the pilot a sense of security. This is done by proper briefing, giving him an accurate knowledge of the existing flak installations, making arrangements for flak spotters, whose job it is to neutralise the flak, and to assign adequate top cover for the operation.

The actual technique of attack depends on the target, but it varies only in method of approach and breakaway, the firing run being the same in all cases. An undefended target of opportunity is of course the simplest, and pilots should be taught to take their time and concentrate on shooting. The most effective pass is one that is steep enough to carry the pilot above most of the obstacles in the line of flight, yet not so steep as to cause him to gain so much speed as to make him apprehensive about pulling out.

Experience has shown that if the pass is too steep pilots will fire out of range, and be forced to pull out just when they are getting into good shooting distance. I believe that a 20-degree dive to the target will produce the best results. In such a dive, the pilot should have his aeroplane trimmed and his sight on the target so as to allow him to commence firing at a range of 500 yards. From this point, the attack can be pressed home, and all the

CO of the 353rd FG's 352nd FS from its formation in October 1942 through to 7 July 1944, Lt Col William Bailey finished the war as one of the most experienced pilots in the ETO. Transferring to the group's HQ flight following his marathon stint with the 352nd FS, he had flown 186 missions (454.05 hours) by VE-Day. Bailey's final wartime tally was three aerial and three strafing victories (*via Graham Cross*)

A beautiful shot of *Double Trouble*, the first P-51D (44-14303) flown by former 352nd FS CO Lt Col Bill Bailey. The P-47 in the background suggests that this picture was taken soon after the 353rd FG had converted to the Mustang, by which time Bailey had transferred to the group's HQ flight. The four kill markings beneath the cockpit means that this photograph was snapped sometime after 4 August 1944, when Bailey claimed two He 111s and a Ju 88 destroyed on the ground during an attack on Plantlunne. He almost certainly used this machine to claim these victories

bullets should go straight into the target at the initial point of opening fire.

The conduct of your aircraft prior to the firing pass, and on the breakaway, is governed by the opposition encountered. On a heavily defended target, such as an airdrome, I favour a high speed pass made from 8000 or 10,000 ft, incorporating plenty of turns and skids prior to the firing run. The firing run should be accomplished as outlined above, with the pilot concentrating on one particular target. Rarely will a pilot have a chance to fire effectively at more than one target during a high speed pass.

The breakaway should be accomplished by staying as low as possible until well clear of the target area, followed by a rapid climb back to 8000 or 10,000 ft. On this type of target, two aircraft can make a simultaneous pass, but I am not in favour of using more than two, as they are too vulnerable.

The main point to remember is that when a pilot fires he should be on his target. Three seconds of fire in one spot will do the work, and the spraying of bullets over, under and around the target is of no value. The proper technique is to hold your fire until you know you're going to hit the bull's eye, and then put your whole burst into it.

COL THOMAS J J CHRISTIAN JR
COMMANDING OFFICER
361st FG

This report represents the composite opinion of the entire 361st FG . All of the pilots of this group do not necessarily concur in the opinions expressed herein, but I believe the majority are in accord.

Usually, a successful fighter attack against a ground target requires less skill, more nerve, and as precise an estimate of the situation as an air-to-air attack. We say *usually*, because there are exceptions. For example, successful fighter-bombing is a specialised sport which requires considerable practice and skill. Moreover, it does not take any courage to shoot up an undefended target (provided you know beforehand that the target *is* undefended), and it is often much easier to make a proper estimate of a ground situation than it is to make one of an air situation because, in many cases, we are afforded prior knowledge of the target conditions. The latter is never true in air-to-air combat.

STRAFING ATTACK AGAINST AIRDROMES

The most successful attack that this group has made against a ground target occurred on 29 June 1944 at Oschersleben airdrome. The mission that day was an escort job to B-24s which were to bomb Oschersleben airdrome. One squadron briefed itself to attack the field after the bombers bombed. The attack was made by the squadron leader and his flight as planned. Coming down through the smoke and fire caused by the bombing, the flight failed to see any aircraft on the first pass. As they went back to shoot up some trucks south of the field, they noticed aeroplanes on the field. Since there was no flak, although a great deal of smoke caused by the bombing, the four aeroplanes flew a gunnery pattern from east to west down a straight line of approximately 20 Fw 190s and a total of 45 to 50 other aeroplanes scattered around the field.

The flight flew in string formation, each man picking an individual target and firing at it. Eight passes were made in all. When ammunition began to run low, the flight pulled off and rejoined the bombers. A conservative estimate placed the damage at 16 destroyed and eight damaged.

Col Thomas J J Christian Jr was the highly-respected CO of the 361st FG, which went into action in January 1944. Having started the war flying B-17s with the 19th BG from Clark Field, in the Philippines, Christian had retrained as a fighter pilot following his evacuation from Bataan to Australia. Transferred to the 67th FS, and flying P-39 and P-400 Airacobras, he flew 60 hours of combat over Guadalcanal between September and November 1942, before being rotated back to the USA. Given command of the newly-formed 361st FG in February 1943, Christian led the group to Britain in November of that same year. A highly respected combat leader, he remained in the vanguard of the group's operations until his death in combat on the afternoon of 14 August 1944. Leading the 361st's fourth, and final, mission of the day, Christian headed for Arras to dive-bomb the marshalling yards in the French town. He had mentioned to his pilots in the pre-mission briefing that he was concerned with the group's poor dive-bombing accuracy, and he decided to show them how it should be done. Christian's P-51D (44-13410) was the first of the 24 Mustangs sortied by the 361st FG to dive on the target, but instead of pulling out, he disappeared into the smoke and haze over Arras and hit the ground at high speed. With little flak opposing the 361st on this mission, it is believed that Col Christian's Mustang either suffered mechanical failure, or the pilot dived too close to the target and the concussion of his bombs exploding crippled his fighter. The destruction of the P-51 was total, and Thomas Christian's final resting place was an unnamed grave in a British cemetery near Arras

In evaluating this attack, the following points are noteworthy. The squadron briefed itself on this airdrome even though its primary mission was bomber-escort. The squadron leader timed his attack to hit the field when the flak defences were at their most disorganised. The flight was able to fly in string formation because there was no flak to worry about. Ordinarily, string formation is not considered good for more than one pass, and preferably not even one pass. The flight did not use up all of its ammunition because it was still deep in enemy territory. Many fighters from our own and other groups were providing general area top cover for the strafing flight.

FIGHTER-BOMBER ATTACKS AGAINST TRANSPORTATION TARGETS

On all fighter-bomber missions, we believe that a thorough and proper briefing is all important. This is best illustrated by two of our missions during the first week of the invasion. On the first mission, we were assigned a small area west of Chateaudun within which to bomb and strafe rail transportation. Our volumes listing tactical targets covered only one-half of the area, and only one of the two obvious rail junctions. The rail junction at Courtalain was recommended by Group Intelligence as the primary target because a good illustration was available, and it was only five miles due east of Chateaudun and its airdrome, which could serve as a good check point. Two secondary targets were also selected.

The leader briefed the target area from the 1:50,000 folio map, showing the illustration to his other seven pilots. The weather included nine-tenths of low clouds with 5000 ft ceiling, reduced by showers to 2000 ft. The two flights successfully found the target, exploded an ammunition train at the primary, and scored six hits on the yard and rails at this important junction. All aeroplanes returned. Low altitude dive-bombing was used on this target.

The second most successful dive-bombing mission occurred on 11 June 1944 in the same area. Twenty-four pilots were briefed for this mission, and the rail junction at Chateau-Du-Loir was picked as the primary target. Briefing was extremely hurried, and all aeroplanes were airborne one hour after receiving the Field Order. The weather was ten-tenths middle cloud between 8500 and 9500 ft and five- to seven-tenths low cloud between 2500 to 6000 ft, with considerable haze above 2500 ft. Two squadrons bombed the primary, destroyed the roundhouse by glide-bombing 'right in the front door', damaged eight to ten locomotives in the front repair area, left 20 goods wagons burning and broke the track in many places. The third squadron followed the railroad south and dive-bombed a string of 100 box and flat cars loaded with armoured vehicles. Fifteen were destroyed.

We consider that the success of the above two missions was due in the main to a good, even though hurried, briefing, and to excellent navigation in very poor weather.

ON ATTACKING AIRDROMES

If the attack is planned well in advance, and the group has time to conduct a thorough briefing and has only one airdrome as the specific target, I believe that coordinated passes may be made with comparative safety by not more than two eight-ship sections. These sections should make their passes from different directions, and timed as close together as possible. One squadron of 16 aeroplanes makes a good top cover.

To aid in the element of surprise, which is all important in a mission of this type, we believe the top cover squadron should circle at some distance from the target, arriving over the target a few minutes later. The lead flight of the other two sections should have their aeroplanes line abreast within flights, in close trail, maintaining a minimum speed of 325 mph. After the pass, evasive action should be taken by staying on the deck, skidding and keeping up air speed until a few miles past the target, at which time altitude should be regained and sections reformed. Any evidence of flak should be immediately called out by the top cover. If the target is of sufficient importance to warrant the employment of at least 16 aeroplanes as indicated, we believe that it will usually be defended by so much flak that a second pass is not advisable.

When an airdrome target of opportunity presents itself while the group is on escort, or returning from a mission, it is our belief that such airdromes as are in line with the bombers' track have been thoroughly alerted long before the fighters or bombers approach the immediate vicinity. In such cases, it is advisable to use only one flight, or, at the most, one section. Either one of two types of attacks are made – the flight or section dives from altitude straight toward the target, making its pass at a speed of 450 mph or faster, or else the flight or section passes by the field, letting down some distance away and, taking advantage of any available terrain features, approaches the airdrome on the deck at a speed of around 400 mph. In both situations only one pass is advisable, and a flight should be placed at medium altitude as top cover, observers, or to draw the airdrome gunners' attention away from the approaching strafers.

A few pilots in this group believe that strafing airdromes is not worth the time, trouble or material expended, with the possible exception of hitting an airdrome immediately being attacked by bombers. The point here is that we should not attack a well defended airdrome *unless the profit is going to be worth the risk*.

DIVE-BOMBING

We are in favour of bombing with fighter aircraft, but recommend that nothing weighing less than a 500-lb bomb be used. The average bridge encountered in occupied territory can usually be damaged by skip-bombing with a 500-lb bomb and a delayed action fuse. Dive-bombing is much too inaccurate for pinpoint targets. Our fighter-bombers have been very accurate in cutting railways by glide-bombing with 500-lb bombs fitted with four-second delayed fuses. Marshalling yards, having a concentration of freight cars, have been dive-bombed successfully. We still believe that a flight of B-24s can do more damage to an airfield by bombing than a group of fighters can do by dive-bombing, however.

It must be remembered that in skip-bombing, the bomb must be skipped into something solid. There have been a few instances in this group where 250- and 500-lb bombs were skipped into locomotives and freight cars, but due to the speed and weight of the bombs, they went right through the target and exploded harmlessly in adjacent fields. After releasing their bombs, pilots must take immediate evasive action by turning sharply to the right or left, otherwise they stand a chance of being blown up by their own bombs which may skip along underneath the aeroplane.

AREA STRAFING – TRANSPORTATION TARGETS

In the past, strafing areas have usually been designated by Fighter Command Orders. On missions of this type, an attempt is made in a thorough briefing to present a clear picture of the plan of attack to all pilots. It is difficult to present a specific plan or course to be followed, but pilots are impressed with the importance of keeping the squadron together at all times during this sort of mission. At briefing, the main railroads and roads in the area are pointed out to the pilots. Flak areas are also indicated.

Generally speaking, flak can be expected at, or near, all airfields, in large towns (especially in the vicinity of marshalling yards), at approaches to large bridges, occasionally at railroad tunnel approaches, and a few other spots such as large factories and power plants. Because of the constant possibility of unexpectedly running into light gun positions while on the deck, and also the possibility of being bounced, it is important that a steady, high air speed of not less than 250 mph be maintained.

One squadron normally patrols the area at medium altitude to provide top cover. The remaining two squadrons are briefed as to what courses and part of the area they will cover – i.e., if there are definite geographical or other check points in the area, such as main roads or railroads, or rivers, one squadron will cover one side of the river or railroad, while the second squadron shoots up targets on the other side. Squadrons on the deck fly at anywhere from 500 to 2000 ft in line abreast formation within flights, and flights in train. R/T discipline and courtesy while flying on this type of a mission is as important to the success of the mission as good shooting. Pilots calling out targets of opportunity, or important information, should be clear and specific with their information, and should always identify themselves.

Generally speaking, flight leaders are free to lead their flights on any available targets they may come across. If the last flight stays behind to finish off a target, the squadron leader should not get too far ahead before he starts his orbit to wait for trailing flights. Flights generally attack in string when firing on an undefended ground target. A set traffic pattern should be maintained within the flight.

GENERAL

Recommend the use of more incendiary ammunition, together with API, for all ground target missions.

Against a target that may explode, it is a good idea to fire a short burst from quite a distance away, aiming rather high. This may be enough to explode the target. If not, then fire a long burst, aiming a little high, watch for hits, and then lead fire into the target. There is no need to press an attack to within 25 ft of the target (locos, munitions trains, etc.). Two aeroplanes of this group were lost by flying through explosions caused by their own gunfire.

For inter-fighter-group R/T, advise using the names of towns, rather than code letters, for check points.

Pilots should save about 50 rounds per gun during strafing missions. In the P-51D, a pilot can expend all the ammunition in his outboard guns and still have enough left in the two inboards to engage in combat if necessary.

Good strafing pictures provide a great incentive for many pilots. The camera mounts in the P-51 are poor, and should be made steadier.

If there is a low overcast or considerable cloud, top cover is not very effective. Sections of a squadron can cover each other in this case. It is very difficult to keep track of a squadron if the top cover is more than 8000 ft high. Sections and squadrons flying top cover should trade places with the attacking aeroplanes so as to make maximum use of ammunition.

There is seldom any need to call in another group on a ground-strafing job. Usually, too long a time elapses before another group can get there, or else it is too difficult to direct another group to your position. Our top cover squadron usually calls the location of such targets to the Controller for his information.

The enemy is making use of shadows cast by trees which line almost all French roads. He is using the smaller side roads, the cover of darkness, and such camouflage techniques as painting his vehicles to resemble civilian trucks and piling hay over his equipment. We discovered half-track personnel carriers and gun carriers camouflaged by means of a canvas cover framework. They were painted red or green and had signs on the sides. The half-tracks showed below the canvas cover.

API ammunition has proven quite satisfactory, but it is likely that plain incendiary would ignite some targets much faster.

The value of firing at flak towers is doubtful. They are usually very heavily armoured. Many towers reported as being flak towers are actually water towers, and, for that reason, no fire was visible from them.

We believe that dive-bombing is such a speciality that, in order to get good results on pinpoint targets, special dive-bombing groups should be developed.

An aeroplane has to be about 70 ft high in order to pour out any continuous fire at a target. Both the pop-up before firing and the straight-in pass are used. Against convoys, it has been found better to make a straight and rather steep diving pass. In the latter case, you have better visibility and a better choice of targets.

Always consider the target as being well defended. Use the element of surprise as much as possible. If at all possible, make your attack according to topographic features such as coming in low over a wooded area and departing over a wooded area. The sun and low cloud cover may be used to good advantage.

Most of the anti-aircraft defence information is too old to be of any help. The increasing use of mobile flak has made this problem increasingly difficult.

A few good aerial photos are available, but we would like more oblique shots covering wider areas and, if possible, disclosing something about the relief features of the terrain.

The qualifications for a successful strafing pilot are plenty of daring, the ability to size up a situation and to arrive at a plan of attack quickly and on the spot, and, of course, he must be a cool shot. He must know when not to attack as well as when to attack. Many pilots enjoy ground strafing much more than escort work due to the certainty of action when they start out.

APPENDICES

High Scoring Strafing Aces of VIII Fighter Command

Name	Strafing Score	Aerial Score	Unit/s
Righetti, Elwyn G, Lt Col	27	7.5	55th FG
Thury, Joseph L, Lt Col	25.5	2.5	339th FG
Landers, John D, Lt Col	20	14.5	55th, 78th & 357th FGs
Tower, Archie A, Maj	18	1.5	339th FG
Kinnard, Claiborne H, Lt Col	17	8	4th, 355th & 356th FGs
Compton, Gordon B, Capt	15	5.5	353rd FG
Cullerton, William J, Lt	15	5	355th FG
Goodson, James A, Maj	15	14	4th FG
Brown, Henry W, Capt	14.5	14.2	355th FG
Glover, Fred W, Maj	14.5	10.333	4th FG
Heller, Edwin L, Capt	14.5	5.5	352nd FG
Hightshoe, Melville W, Capt	14.5	0	353rd FG
Kolb, Herbert G, Capt	14.5	0	353rd FG
Montgomery, Gerald E, Maj	14.5	3	4th FG
Godfrey, John T, Maj	13.67	16.333	4th FG
Hofer, Ralph K, Lt	13.5	15	4th FG
Elder, John L, Lt Col	13	8	355th FG
Everson, Kirke B, Capt	13	1.5	339th FG
Littge, Raymond H, Capt	13	10.5	352nd FG
Meyer, John C, Lt Col	13	24	352nd FG
Gustke, Richard N, Flt Off	12.5	0	353rd FG
Welch, Robert E, Capt	12	6	55th FG
Boone, Walker L, Maj	11.79	2	78th & 353rd FGs
Biggs, Oscar K, Lt	11.5	0.5	339th FG

Name	Strafing Score	Aerial Score	Unit/s
Burch, Harold W, Lt	11	0	339th FG
Corey, Harry R, Capt	11	1	339th FG
Lanoue, Roland J, Lt	11	1	353rd FG
Miller, Gerald J, Lt	11	0	353rd FG
Murphy, Randel L, Lt	11	2	56th FG
Olds, Robin, Maj	11	13	479th FG
Schilling, David C, Col	10.5	22.5	56th FG
Emory, Frank N, Capt	10	2	353rd FG
McMullen, Joseph D, Lt	10	0	353rd FG
Morris, Ray S, Lt	10	3.5	355th FG
Graham, Gordon M, Lt Col	9.5	7	355th FG
Olson, Thomas C, Lt	9.5	1	479th FG
Ammon, Robert H, Capt	9	5	339th FG
Anderson, Woodrow W, Capt	9	4.5	352nd FG
Duffy, James E, Capt	9	5.25	355th FG
Johnson, Martin H, Capt	9	1	361st FG
Lowell, John H, Lt Col	9	7.5	364th FG
Malmsten, Donald M, Capt	9	1.5	4th FG
Marvel, Thomas W, Lt	9	0	339th FG
McCormick, Arthur C, Capt	9	1	364th FG
Taylor, Clyde E, Lt	9	0	78th FG
Duffie, Claire A P, Maj	8.5	3	479th FG
Gilbert, Olin E, Lt Col	8.5	2	78th FG & 66th FW
Pierce, Donald J, Capt	8.5	0	4th, 479th FGs
Zemke, Hubert, Col	8.5	17.75	56th & 479th FGs
Alfred, Carl R, Capt	8	0	4th FG
Clark, William C, Col	8	1	66th FW & 339th FG
Falvey, Harold W, Flt Off	8	0	355th FG
Harrington, Frances E, Lt	8	4	78th FG

Colour Plates

Aircraft flown by a number of the leading P-47 and P-51 strafing aces do not appear in this colour section due to the fact that their fighters have already featured in profile in *Aircraft of the Aces 1 - Mustang Aces of the Eighth Air Force*, *Aircraft of the Aces 18 - Lightning Aces of the ETO/MTO*, *Aircraft of the Aces 24 - P-47 Thunderbolt Aces of the Eighth Air Force*, *Aviation Elite 2 - 56th Fighter Group*, *Aviation Elite 8 - 352nd Fighter Group* or *Aviation Elite 10 - 359th Fighter Group*.

1

P-47D-11 42-75237/*WHACK!!* of Lt Col Dave Schilling, Deputy CO of the 56th FG, Halesworth, February 1944

David Schilling's third Thunderbolt in the ETO replaced P-47D 42-7938 in late January 1944. As with his previous fighters, the 56th FG's Deputy CO had 42-75237 adorned with another version of his favoured 'Hairless Joe' motif, which was a character from the *Lil' Abner* comic strip which regularly featured in the *Stars and Stripes* service newspaper. *Whack!!* was more an exclamation than a name for the Thunderbolt. As far as is known, Schilling only shot down one enemy aircraft flying this P-47, but at least three more were claimed by other pilots who flew it – none of Schilling's 10.5 strafing kills were claimed in this aircraft. In May 1944, when Schilling acquired another P-47, 42-75237 became LM-S. Later transferred to the 61st FS, it was lost to flak near Koln on 5 September 1944, pilot Lt Earl Hertel successfully evading capture.

2

P-47D-15 42-75864 of Col Hubert Zemke, CO of the 56th FG, Halesworth, March 1944

This modified P-47D was assigned to Col Hubert Zemke when he returned from the USA in January 1944. The CO used this fighter to obtain two-and-a-quarter aerial victories (and a probable) over German fighters on 6 March 1944, and two days later Dave Schilling was flying it when he damaged an Fw 190. It was also used by both Zemke and Schilling to claim their first strafing kills, on 11 February and 8 March 1944 respectively. On 16 March the aircraft was completely destroyed when a fierce blaze broke out during a maintenance start-up at the 56th FG's Halesworth home.

3

P-47D-21 42-25506/*Dove of Peace VI* of Col Glenn Duncan, CO of the 353rd FG, Raydon, April 1944

Glenn Duncan joined the 353rd FG in March 1943, and was its CO from November 1943 through to July 7 1944. He scored his first aerial victory, over an Fw 190, on 23 September 1943, and became an aerial ace by downing another Fw 190 on 20 December 1943. He was shot down by flak on 7 July 1944, but survived to join the Dutch underground, before ultimately returning to his unit in April 1945. His total score was 19.5 aerial and 6.833 strafing victories. 42-25506 was the very first 'silver' P-47D received by the 353rd FG, and it was replaced by the identically-marked 42-25971 (distinguished by the application of a small Roman VII alongside the X) following a landing accident at Copdock, near Ipswich. Lt Carl W Mueller of the 350th FS was flying the aircraft at the time, and he was forced to belly it in following engine trouble minutes after taking off

on a fighter-bomber mission on 27 April 1944. The fighter was salvaged, rather than repaired. Duncan did not get the chance to add to his growing tally in this machine prior to its premature demise. The 353rd FG CO briefly named one of his P-47s *"Flying Death"* in early 1944, but was quickly ordered by VIII Fighter Command HQ to remove it for fear of the political implications should the aircraft be shot down and captured intact. Duncan sarcastically renamed it, and all of his subsequent mounts, *Dove of Peace*!

4

P-51D-5 44-13303 of Maj James Goodson, 336th FS/ 4th FG, Debden, June 1944

Goodson was a member of the RAF's No 133 'Eagle' Sqn when it became the 4th FG's 336th FS in September 1942. He scored his first aerial victory, over an Fw 190, on 22 June 1943, and became an aerial ace on 7 January 1944 while flying a P-47. Goodson was also an early strafing ace as well, destroying two Ju 88s on 29 March near Brunswick to take his tally to five kills – he was flying the P-51B by then. Goodson continued his good run on 5 April 1944 when he claimed three and three shared strafing victories at Stendal. Five days later he was credited with another five and one shared on the ground during an attack on Romorantin, in France. Eventually shot down by flak while attacking Neubrandenberg airfield, in Germany, on 20 June 1944 in the 44-13303, Goodson, who was CO of the 336th FS at the time of his demise, spent the rest of the war in captivity.

5

P-51D-5 44-13537/*Sweet Thing IV* of Lt Col Roy Webb, 374th FS/361st FG, Bottisham, June 1944

The first CO of the 374th FS, Roy Webb opened his aerial account with a Bf 109 kill on 30 January 1944 whilst flying a P-47. One of four victories claimed by his unit on this day, these would be the first of 221 aerial kills credited to the 361st FG by war's end. Webb's fourth, and final, aerial victory came on 25 June 1944 when he shot down an Fw 190 in newly-delivered 44-13537 south of Caen. Four days later he claimed all five of his strafing victories (again in 44-13537) during a strafing attack on Oschersleben airfield. Webb was posted to a desk job at Eighth Air Force HQ in August, having completed his tour upon reaching 300 combat hours.

6

P-38J-15 42-38393/*Wrangler* of Col Cy Wilson, CO of the 20th FG, Kings Cliffe, June 1944

Cy Wilson joined the 20th FG in April 1944 as CO of the 55th FS following the death of the previous incumbent, Maj Donald McAuley, during a strafing attack on Chateaudun airfield on 23 April. Promoted to group CO on 25 June upon the transferring out of the tour-expired Col Harry Rau, Wilson celebrated his promotion by achieving his first aerial victory (a Bf 109) that same day south of Paris. He quickly gained a reputation for being one of the foremost 'train-busters' of the Eighth Air Force, using the P-38's nose-mounted 20 mm AN-M2 'C' cannon and four 0.50-cal Browning machine guns to good effect. Wilson also claimed three aerial kills. Overseeing the conversion of his unit to the P-51 in late July 1944, Wilson was hit by flak (in P-51D 44-13951 *Wrangler Jr*) whilst escorting bombers over Denmark on 27 August and forced to bale out off the coast. He was soon rescued and spent the rest of the war as a PoW. Wilson had completed 78 missions and 318.40 combat hours by the time of his demise.

7

P-51B-10 42-106437 of Lt Ray S 'Silky' Morris, 354th FS/355th FG, Steeple Morden, July 1944

One of five pilots within the 355th FG to score ten or more strafing kills, Ray 'Silky' Morris of the 354th FS saw combat in the ETO from October 1943 through to July 1944, when he completed his 74-mission tour. During that time he claimed 3.5 aerial and ten strafing kills, all with the P-51B. Morris scored his first aerial victory on 16 March 1944 and subsequently became one of the 'Steeple Morden Strafers', being credited with the destruction of four aircraft during April 1944 and another three on 24 June. The bulk of these claims were scored in this aircraft, which was his only assigned Mustang.

8

P-47D-25 42-26413/ "OREGONS BRITANNIA" of Col Hubert Zemke, CO of the 56th FG, Boxted, August 1944

This Thunderbolt was the last example assigned to 'Hub' Zemke prior to his departure from the 56th to take command of the 479th FG on 12 August 1944. Bearing the War Bond inscription "OREGONS BRITANNIA", it was used by Zemke to score six aerial and 2.5 strafing kills. Following the 'Hub's' departure to the 479th, this aircraft was flown by five-victory ace Harold Comstock (and several other pilots), who had been CO of the 63rd FS since 19 July 1944. Comstock had the legend HAPPY WARRIOR added to the veteran fighter in celebration of his promotion to major on 17 September 1944. Used by Comstock to claim two aerial and two strafing kills, 42-26413 was finally written off when Lt Sam Batson (who also downed two aircraft with the veteran fighter) stalled in after suffering an engine failure whilst on approach to landing at Boxted following a local flight on 30 December 1944. Batson, who had flown 21 missions since his arrival in the ETO in October 1944, perished in the crash.

9

P-47D-28 44-19790/ Teddy of Capt Michael Jackson, 62nd FS/56th FG, Boxted, November 1944

Capt Michael Jackson was assigned 44-19790 in mid-September 1944, and he flew it until receiving a P-47M in February 1945. Teddy entered service with a Dark Green and Light Sea Gray disruptive pattern on the uppersurfaces, which was the commonest form of 'in-the-field' camouflage applied to 62nd FS aircraft. The undersurfaces remained in natural metal finish. Jackson, who scored five of his eight aerial victories in this aircraft, had both his air and ground strafing destroyed credits (5.5 in total) painted below the cockpit of Teddy – his aerial victories took the form of white outlined crosses. Jackson's solitary strafing kill in this machine was an Me 262 destroyed at Neuburg on 4 December 1944. He damaged a second jet and an Fw 200 on the same mission.

10

P-51D-15 44-14787 of Maj Fred W Glover, 336th FS/4th FG, Debden, November 1944

Glover trained in the RAF and joined the 336th FS in February

1944. His first aerial victories were scored on 16 June 1944 when he shot down two Bf 110s, becoming an ace on 3 August. Glover destroyed his first enemy aircraft on the ground on 5 April 1944, but scored most of his ground victories the following year, including three on 16 January and another three on 27 February. His total score was 10.333 in the air and 12.5 on the ground. Glover claimed four aerial and at least three strafing kills in 44-14787.

11

P-51D-10 44-14402/ BARBARA of Capt Fred R Haviland, 357th FS/355th FG, Steeple Morden, November 1944

Haviland joined the 355th FG in June 1944, and on the 21st of that month he downed his first aircraft (a Bf 109). He scored his fifth and six kills (an Fw 190 and a Bf 109) on 26 November in 44-14402, which were his final successes in the ETO. Haviland also claimed six strafing victories, three on 24 June and three on 12 September. Although he failed to achieve any confirmed strafing kills in 44-14402, he was credited with damaging four Me 262s at Leipheim on 18 November.

12

P-51D-10 44-14292/ Man O'War of Col Claiborne Kinnard, CO of the 4th FG, Debden, November 1944

Kinnard spent most of his time with the 355th FG, although he transferred to 4th FG as Deputy CO in early September 1944, and took over the group from Col Don Blakeslee on the 15th of that same month. Already an ace with five aerial and 11.5 strafing kills by the time he arrived at Debden, Kinnard claimed a further one aerial (a Bf 109 on 11 September) and three ground kills (an Me 410 on 11 September and two Hs 123s two days later) flying this particular fighter with the 4th FG. Returning to the 355th FG as CO in November 1944, Kinnard added two aerial and 2.5 strafing kills to his tally in April 1945, taking his final tally to eight aerial and 17 strafing victories. He had at least four assigned Mustangs during his time in the ETO, three of which were named Man O' War.

13

P-51D-10 44-14419/ "Janie" of Capt Bill Price, 350th FS/353rd FG, Raydon, December 1944

An original member of the 353rd FG's 350th FS, Price flew two tours with the group between November 1942 and December 1944. He completed 108 missions in the ETO, scoring two aerial and four strafing victories flying P-47s, and a solitary air-to-air kill in this Mustang. He was Deputy CO of the 350th FS between August and October 1944, during which time the unit scored 40 aerial and strafing victories.

14

P-51D-20 44-63684/ Double Trouble Two of Lt Col William B Bailey, 353rd FG, Raydon, February 1945

CO of the 353rd FG's 352nd FS from its formation in October 1942 through to 7 July 1944, William Bailey finished the war as one of the most experienced pilots in the ETO. Transferring to the group's HQ flight following his marathon stint with the 352nd FS, he had flown 186 missions (454.05 hours) by VE-Day. Bailey's final wartime tally was three aerial and three strafing victories. Although he claimed no strafing kills in this particular Mustang, he almost certainly 'bagged' two Fw 190s with it south of Wittenburg on 2 March 1945. These were Bailey's final kills of the war

15

P-51D-10 44-14696/*HELL-ER-BUST* of Capt Edwin L Heller, 486th FS/352nd FG, Bodney, April 1945

The 352nd FG's ranking strafing ace with 16.5 kills, Ed Heller also enjoyed success in aerial engagements too, scoring 5.5 victories. A veteran of some 520 combat hours in the ETO during the course of two tours, Heller was assigned at least one P-47 and two P-51s during his time with the 352nd, and 44-14696 was the last of these. Issued to him in November 1944, he added one aerial and seven strafing kills to his tally with the Mustang in just two actions. Heller claimed an Fw 190 shot down south-east of Leipzig on 2 March 1945, and three Fw 190s, two Ju 87s, a Bf 109 and an unidentified trainer were destroyed on the ground at Ganacker on 16 April 1945. Serving in the USAF post-war, he saw further combat in Korea, where he shot down three MiG-15s before being downed himself and spending the rest of the war in captivity.

16

P-51D-15 44-15326/*Sizzlin' Liz* of Maj Gerald Montgomery, 334th FS/4th FG, Debden, March 1945

Montgomery flew two tours with the 4th FG, and scored his first aerial victory on 14 January 1944 when he downed an Fw 190. In March and April 1944 he became a successful ground strafer, destroying seven aircraft. Montgomery enjoyed more strafing success in 1945 when he destroyed a Bf 108, a Ju 87 and a Do 217 on the ground at Weimar on 27 February, followed by a solitary Me 410 at Wittstock on 10 April. These final four kills were all claimed in 44-15326, which Montgomery replaced with 44-72382 just prior to VE-Day. His final tally was three aerial and 14.5 strafing kills.

17

P-47M-1 44-21114/*MIM* of Lt Col Lucian 'Pete' Dade, CO of the 56th FG, Boxted, March 1945

Initially the personal mount of group commanding officer Lt Col 'Pete' Dade, 44-21114 was later reassigned to Lt Fred Polansky. It is highly probable that Dade destroyed three of his six strafing kills with this aircraft during the 56th FG's devastating attack on Eggebeck airfield on 13 April 1945. As with all operational P-47Ms of the 62nd FS, the aircraft had its uppersurfaces camouflaged in a disruptive pattern of Dark Green and Light Sea Gray. Undersurfaces were unpainted, and the code letters and tail number were in Insignia Yellow. P-47Ms reaching the unit after VE-Day were not camouflaged.

18

P-47M-1 44-21141/*"the Brat"* of Lt Randel Murphy, 63rd FS/56th FG, Boxted, April 1945

Assigned to Lt Randel Murphy, this was the aircraft in which he claimed the destruction of ten enemy aircraft by strafing on 13 April 1945 – a USAAF record for one mission. It wears the standard 63rd FS camouflage for P-47Ms, namely a disruptive pattern of what is believed to be Dark Mediterranean Blue and Azure Blue on the uppersurfaces, with a sky blue rudder and tail number. The code letters were left as bare aluminium, and polished for silver sheen effect. Undersurfaces and wing leading edges remained unpainted.

19

P-51D-10 44-14314/*PRUNE FACE* of Maj Henry S Bille, 357th FS/355th FG, Steeple Morden, March 1945

A two-tour ETO veteran who joined the 355th FG in February 1943, and stayed with it through to VE-Day, Henry Bille's first aerial victory was scored over a Bf 109 on 13 April 1944. He became an aerial ace (one of the Eighth Air Force's last), when he shot down two more on 20 April 1945. Bille achieved all his ground victories on VIII Fighter Command's big day, 16 April 1945. Bille's total score was six aerial and four strafing kills, and all of the latter, as well as his ace-making double on 20 April, were claimed in 44-14314.

20

P-51D-10 44-14004/*Annie Mae* of Lt Robert H Ammon, 503rd FS/339th FG, Fowlmere, April 1945

Robert Ammon completing two combat tours with the 339th FG's 503rd FS, scoring aerial victories in June (one) and September (four) 1944. All his strafing kills came on 16 April 1945, when he claimed a record 11 enemy aircraft destroyed on the ground at Prague/Kbely – he was subsequently credited with nine victories. Ammon was flying this aircraft on the 16 April sortie, the Mustang bearing the titling *Annie Mae* on its starboard side.

21

P-51D-20 44-72449/*IMOGENE* of Lt Oscar K Biggs, 505th FS/339th FG, Fowlmere, April 1945

Although nowhere near as experienced as group mate Bob Ammon, Oscar Biggs nevertheless made his mark on the 16 April attack on Prague/Kbely airfield by scoring three kills to add to his other strafing victories on 1 and 2 March and 7 and 10 April 1945. Biggs took his final tally to 0.5 aerial and 11.5 strafing kills on 17 April. Having only arrived in the ETO in February 1945, his solitary mount during his five months with the 339th FG was 44-72449.

22

P-51D-10 44-14561/*MISS VELMA* of Capt Frank Birtciel, 343rd FS/55th FG, Wormingford, April 1945

Assigned to the 55th FG just a month prior to the group's departure for the UK in September 1943, Frank Birtciel completed 121 missions with the 343rd FS through to April 1945. He claimed all five of his strafing kills on 9 April 1945 (in 44-14561), when the 55th attacked Munich-Brunnthal airfield.

23

P-51K-5 44-11678/*Bobby Jeanne* of Lt Col Irwin Dregne, CO of the 357th FG, Leiston, April 1945

The final CO of the 357th FG (from 2 December 1944), Irwin Dregne had transferred to the group from the 363rd FG in May 1943. Flying with the HQ flight throughout his time in the ETO, Dregne claimed five aerial and 5.5 strafing kills. All of his successes in 1945 came in this P-51K, one aerial and four strafing victories being credited to him in January and April. Amongst the latter were two Me 262s and an Fw 190 destroyed at Neuruppin on 10 April.

24

P-51D-20 44-63764/*DRAGON WAGON* of Capt Jim Duffy, 354th FS/355th FG, Steeple Morden, April 1944

Duffy flew two combat tours with the 355th FG, scoring his first kill in a P-47 when he downed an Fw 190 on 21 January 1944. He achieved aerial ace status just over a year later on 9 February 1945 when he destroyed his fifth Fw 190 whilst flying 44-63764. He also claimed the last five of his nine strafing kills in this aircraft.

25
P-51D-10 44-14372/*Mary Beth* of Capt Kirke B Everson, 504th FS/339th FG, Fowlmere, April 1945
Another late arrival in the ETO, Everson commenced his tour in February 1945 and enjoyed great success in this aircraft during the numerous airfield strafing missions of April. Sharing in the destruction of an Me 262 over Parchim on 4 April, he scored his only other aerial kill three days later when he downed a Bf 109 near Celle. Three strafing victories followed on 10 April during the Neuruppin attack, and three Fw 190s were destroyed at Klatovy on the 16th. The following day Everson claimed his final seven strafing kills when Klatovy-Anberg was worked over by the 504th FS.

26
P-51D-20 44-63633 of Lt Col John L Elder Jr, 357th FS/355th FG, Steeple Morden, April 1945
One of the 355th's original pilots, John 'Moon' Elder became CO of the 357th FS in July 1944, and remained in command until VE-Day. The squadron's most successful pilot, he claimed eight aerial and thirteen strafing victories, a number of which were scored in this aircraft.

27
P-51D-15 44-15373 of Maj Norman Fortier, 354th FS/355th FG, Steeple Morden, April 1945
Fortier flew two tours with the 355th FG, becoming an aerial ace on 20 July 1944. During his service he flew a B- and two D-model Mustangs, all coded WR-N. Fortier's total score was 5.833 aerial and 5.5 strafing kills, with four of the latter claimed in this aircraft.

28
P-51D-15 44-14966/*Luscious Lu* of Lt Robert L Garlich, 357th FS/355th FG, Steeple Morden, April 1945
Posted to the 355th FG in November 1944, Robert Garlich was one of many pilots from the group to achieve strafing 'acedom' in the April 1945 strafing attacks on Luftwaffe airfields. He destroyed five enemy aircraft that month in 44-14966, taking his final score to 6.5 strafing victories.

29
P-51D-15 44-14985/*The Millie G* of Maj Edward B Giller, 343rd FS/55th FG, Wormingford, April 1945
A 115-mission (420 combat hours) veteran who had served with the 55th FG since February 1943, Ed Giller destroyed some 92 locomotives whilst flying P-38s and P-51s. CO of the 343rd FS at war's end, his final score was three aerial and six strafing kills, all of the latter being scored in April 1945.

30
P-51D-20 44-64148 *Happy IV/Dolly* of Lt Col William C Clark, 339th FG, Fowlmere, April 1945
Deputy CO of the 339th FG, and formerly CO of the 504th FS,

William C Clark became a strafing 'ace in a day' in this aircraft when he destroyed six enemy aircraft during the attack on Klatovy on 16 April 1945. He finished the war with one aerial and eight strafing kills.

31
P-51D-20 44-72216/*Miss HELEN* of Lt Raymond H Littge, 487th FS/352nd FG, Bodney, April 1945
Littge joined the squadron in June 1944 and opened his aerial score on 27 November 1944. He became an aerial ace with the destruction of three Fw 190s on 27 December, and followed that up with an Me 262 on 25 March 1945. His total score was 10.5 aerial and 13 ground victories, many of which were claimed in this aircraft. Still flying today, 44-72216 served with the Swedish and Israeli air forces post-war, and eventually arrived back in the UK in 1976 when bought by its present owner, Robs Lamplough.

32
P-51D-10 44-14359/*Lil Lila Lee* of Capt Joseph E Mellen, 354th FS/355th FG, Steeple Morden, April 1945
After an initial aerial victory on 26 November 1944, Mellen destroyed five aircraft on the ground on 13 April 1945, with an additional three on the 16th to take his score to two aerial and eight strafing kills. All of these victories came in this P-51D.

33
P-51D-10 44-14671 of Lt Col Dale E Shafer, 503rd FS/339th FG, Fowlmere, April 1945
Shafer flew Spitfires with the 31st FG in North Africa in 1943, where he achieved four kills. He joined the 339th FG in August 1944 and became CO of the 503rd FS, increasing his tally to eight aerial and two strafing victories. A solitary aerial victory was claimed in this aircraft on 18 November 1944.

34
P-51D-10 44-14387/*Tar Heel* of Capt James Starnes, 505th FS/339th FG, Fowlmere, April 1945
Starnes arrived in the ETO with the 339th FG in March 1944, and had become an aerial ace by 4 August 1944. A two tour, 113-mission veteran, he flew this particular P-51 from late 1944 until virtually war's end.

35
P-51D-20 44-72437/*Pauline* of Lt Col Joseph Thury, 339th FG, Fowlmere, April 1945
Thury joined the 339th in August 1943 as a member of the 505th FS and flew two combat tours. His first aerial victory was scored on 29 May 1944, having achieved his first two strafing kills 48 hours earlier. His first tour having yielded him two aerial and 9.5 strafing kills, Thury really got amongst the kills in April 1945 when he used 44-72437 to boost his final tally to an incredible 25.5 strafing victories.

36
P-51D-25 44-73074/*"Lucky Boy"* of Maj Archie A Tower, 505th FS/339th FG, Fowlmere, April 1945
Although claiming only two aerial kills, Tower ran up a substantial score of strafing victories. Like Thury, he enjoyed the big missions of April 1945, when he claimed ten ground kills (all in this P-51D) to boost his final score to 18.

127

INDEX

References to illustrations are shown in **bold**. Plates are shown with page and caption locators in brackets.